Photo by Bill Jones

Marvin in Concert

Also by Audrey King Lewis

Fiction

Big Mamma & Celeste

The Gifted

WHY?

(Why did Marvin's father shoot and kill him?)

An authentic account as told to me by his sister, Zeola Gaye

By Audrey King Lewis

Printed and Bound in the United States of America

Cover image	Christopher Schweska
	Joe Lewis
Cover photo	AP Images/Lennox McLendon

Published and Distributed by
Milligan Books,
1425 W. Manchester, Suite C
Los Angeles, California 90047
(323) 750-3592
Website: www.Milliganbooks.com
Email: drrosie@aol.com

First Print, February 2007

ISBN 978-0-9792016-4-6
　　　 0-9792016-4-0

DEDICATION

In loving memory of my late sister, Jeannette, who spent long nights during her illness talking with me on the telephone, allowing me to confide in her all my tears and fears of writing this book. Her encouragement will always be remembered.

Jeannette King Carolina

1938—2006

To Kenneth "Fritzie" Brown who supported me throughout my editing madness.

FOREWORD
BY DR. ROSIE MILLIGAN

The question that continues to plague us all is "Why?" Why did Marvin have to die like he did and why did his father, Marvin Gay Sr. kill him? Audrey Lewis helps to bring closure concerning Marvin's death. She gives to us an authentic inside and close-up view of who Marvin was, how he lived, and why he died, as told to her by Marvin's sister, Zeola Gaye.

I will never forget the gloom that hung over Los Angeles when the news broke that Marvin's father had shot and killed the artist. Marvin's lyrics echoed from the lips of many: What's Going On?"

Marvin was a musical genius; his lyrics were prophetic. He saw the future conditions that plague the world today. Many thought that he had gone over the edge when he recorded one of his last songs, SEXUAL HEALING. Had he gone overboard? I think not, and you will agree as you, too, reflect on the sexual crises which plague us today. As we witness the molestations and sexual crimes from the pulpit to the White House, we now see what Marvin saw. He was a man ahead of his time. He bellowed out prophetic lyrics such as: "taxes too high," "sending our sons to die," "police trigger-happy," etc. All that he sang about is apparent to everyone now and "Makes you want to holler, throw up both your hands." Marvin's music, when played today, continues to bring the young as well as the old to the dance floor.

After reading Audrey's literary work about Marvin, your love for the singer will deepen as you finally get to know the "ins" and "outs" of the real musical genius—Marvin. I want to thank Audrey f or helping to bring closure and resolve to the question asked by the many fans who loved Marvin, "Why?"

PREFACE

In 2001 when Zeola asked me to write this story about her brother, Marvin, I was flattered. Even when she said that she had no money to offer me at that time, I still said that I would consider writing it because I was a big fan of Marvin's.

To me, Marvin was somewhat of a prophet; not in the biblical sense, but in his ability to see what was going on in the world and then be able to write about it with such poetic genius. His inspirational lyrics and inexhaustible musical talent has fueled such enduring hits like WHAT'S GOING ON and SEXUAL HEALING.

Zeola, Marvin's sister, said to me that ever since the shooting in 1984 the most asked question of her has been, *"Why did your father kill your brother?"* She expressed with certainty that she has always known the answer to that question but chose not to deal with it until now. Finally, she said that she is ready to give it up with no holds barred. Before writing this book Zeola and I spoke several times on the telephone. When she told me what she wanted to write about Marvin and her dysfunctional family I knew that it could be very explosive. The blistering intimate details of the super star's personal life are unlike any magazine articles or books that I have been privy to in the past, and there have been many. So I warned Zeola that someone in her family would more than likely try to stop her. I told her that I was concerned that they might even pay her not to reveal the truth as she saw it, but she assured me that that would not happen. *"It's time to let it all out."* She said. *"I want Marvin's fans to know the truth about his life as well as his death."*

Even though I said yes to her offer, I was still concerned with the fact that Zeola's financial situation was such that I felt that if this lady was offered anything that even smelled like cash she might renege on our agreement so I sought legal help, and Zeola signed the papers without hesitation. But even after that I was still concerned about the fact that someone might buy her off before we finished our mission. And they did.

Normally, I guess I should have been angry with her, but I wasn't. By then I had experienced enough spiritual signs of encouragement to continue on my own. Besides, Zeola and I had already recorded numerous hours of both audio and video tape, and I felt that I had enough material to complete Marvin's story. Yes, I call it Marvin's story because ever since I began this assignment, I have been accompanied not only by Zeola, but by a strong and positive life force, which I cannot explain. A spiritual entity that has been encouraging me to finish what I have started. And although the story seems to be Zeola's, I do not believe that it was a coincidence that we were introduced. I believe that we were supposed to do this together. I believe that Marvin is somewhere out there directing me to finish this book.

After months of being incognito, Zeola called me on the telephone and confessed that she had been paid to stop the story. She said that Jan, Marvin's ex-wife had found out about the book and had paid her not to write it. She said that she was about to lose her home so Jan gave her money as well as a place to stay if she would get off drugs and not expose the truth.

Sometimes I think I must feel closer to Marvin's spirit than some family members because nobody could have bought me off for a few dollars if I believed in what I was doing; especially, if it was for someone I claimed to love. Zeola told me many times that she believed in her heart that Marvin wanted her to do this, yet, she chose to sell out for a small amount of money.

Writer, David Ritz said it best when he wrote, *"Marvin never found what he was looking for – acceptance without authority, approval without discipline, love without demands."*

This might explain why nobody close to Marvin heard his cries. Everybody was so busy taking from him that they failed to see the obvious; Marvin needed someone to offer him unconditional help, not to mention his father's unconditional love, something that he never experienced, according to Zeola.

It was then that I began to realize the importance of this story. It is so clear that Marvin died a very sad and lonely person, and I don't believe that it all came from drugs. Of course drugs may have caused some of his confusion, but I have come to believe that his pain and suffering went much deeper than most of us could ever imagine.

There is no doubt that Marvin's eccentric and abusive father, Marvin Gay Sr., pulled the trigger thus being the key to Marvin's untimely demise, but Zeola's idea that Marvin planned this to happen does not set well with me.

After my in-depth tape recorded interviews with her, in addition to talks with people of Marvin's past, my beliefs are that Marvin was simply a deeply confused and sensitive spiritual brother who allowed himself to get caught up in that antagonistic world of drugs and degradation.

I also believe that our beloved musical genius possessed an inconsolable need for his father's love and admiration. In conjunction, it appears that Marvin desperately yearned to be accepted by all for who he truly was, not for what he had become, which was a meal ticket for a group of money hungry drugged out greedy people who hadn't the faintest idea how to reciprocate.

CHAPTER
1

FUNERAL

APRIL 5, 1984 - Media frenzy hovered over and around Hollywood, California. News Helicopters followed the mile long funeral precession of cars up Highland Avenue and along the Hollywood Freeway over to Forest Lawn Drive where crowds of Marvin's fans solemnly waited their turn to view his body at Forest Lawn Cemetery. I remember not wanting to go to the funeral home because I did not want to see the legendary Motown Great in a casket. It was just too much for me to handle at that time, so I watched everything on television.

Emotions ran high as national and local newscasters reported on the shooting and the funeral. Every television network and radio station had tuned in on the funeral procession of long white limousines and was talking about how Marvin had been shot and killed by his father, Marvin Gay Sr., and of course the cameras made sure to include the nearly ten thousand fans lined up along the way.

Simultaneously, footage of Marvin's father being carted off to jail in handcuffs was shown on almost every television network in the country.

It was then I learned that Marvin had added the 'e' to his sir name because he did not like being connected to the word 'gay.'

The media's speculation of the ill-fated shooting ranged from the father's jealousies to allegations that Marvin was on drugs and had beaten his father. I guess the media had not yet learned of Gay Sr.'s supposedly cross-dressing antics or they would have played that up as well.

Some of the television networks reported that there were no witnesses. They stated that Alberta, Marvin's mother, was downstairs, and Frankie, Marvin's brother, was out back in his own apartment behind Gay Sr.'s house aka the 'big house' when the shooting occurred. However, I remember a news reporter stating that Marvin's mother was in the room with Marvin when the shooting took place.

There was so much media hype that day that I could not take myself away from the television. Somehow I felt that if I sat there long enough something would finally make sense of this horrible tragedy. I kept asking myself, like so many others, why this man would shoot and kill his own son; especially when that son was such a great musical genius who literally prophesied to the world through his music. Nothing made any sense to me.

Little did I know that twenty years later I would be once again addressing those same issues, only this time I would be writing about it.

Television cameras captured the pain and devastation on the faces of the well-wishers as they were lined up along the streets watching the hearse quietly and slowly go by. Some were crying while others just held on to each other in disbelief.

I remember sitting and staring motionless at the television in my den. A part of me was glad that I was home alone because the solitude seemed appropriate at the time. I must have sat there for hours. I didn't get up for food or water, or even go to the bathroom. Everything that day seemed so unreal. I think that it was more about disbelief than sorrow. I could not believe that anybody could do something so horrible, especially one's own father, to such a wonderfully talented human being. The sorrow had not yet set in because there was still a part of my brain that had not accepted this senseless killing.

Over time I still did not allow myself to connect with the fact that Marvin was dead because the radios never stopped playing his music, and the television stations never stopped showing clips of his performances. And I never went to the funeral home to view his body. In other words because Marvin's music had never died, his presence, to me, still lived on. True sorrow didn't really set in until about sixteen years later when I first met Zeola, Marvin's youngest sister.

The summer of 2001, I was working as a line producer on a film that was about Marvin, and for some reason I was assigned to go and get Zeola at her home and take her to lunch. I wasn't sure what I was in for because I don't like to make a lot of small talk, especially over lunch with somebody I don't even know. But this was my job assignment so I had to do what I had to do.

Zeola lived on the west side of Los Angeles in a modest three bedroom house located in a nice middle class neighborhood with well manicured lawns and typical pastel colored adobe style houses off the Santa Monica freeway. I had no problems finding her home because I had lived less than a mile from there for about twenty years, and always loved the quiet neighborhood.

The moment I pulled up in front of her house I spotted from my car a huge dog lying on the front porch behind the iron gate. I knew immediately that I was not going up on that porch to ring that doorbell for anybody; not even for Marvin's sister.

After parking my car and sitting there a moment wondering what to do next I decided to call her from my cell phone and ask her to come outside, which she did willingly.

The moment Zeola stepped out of her front door I could see the resemblance between her and Marvin, except I remember thinking how much taller I thought she would be. I suppose that was because I knew that Marvin was tall, and his father appeared to be taller than he really was on television when they took him away after the shooting. Instead, Zeola was a petite and pretty woman in her mid-fifties with short coifed naturally curly hair, big dangly earrings and a beautiful smile very similar to Marvin's smile.

After convincing that bear-like creature of a dog to remain on the porch, she exited her gate and leisurely approached my car with a big black purse tucked under her arm. The moment she headed towards me I found myself somewhat tickled because she had a slow sultry walk that was straight out of an old black and white Mae West movie.

"Hi, you must be Audrey," she greeted with a charismatic smile as she opened the car door on the passenger side and got in and extended her hand to me.

"Yes, I am. It's a pleasure meeting you," I replied and returned the handshake.

But the moment I touched Zeola something strange occurred. A familiar sensation of energy similar to a mild electrical current raced up my arm and to my face. It surprised me at first because I wasn't expecting it, but being that I have had similar encounters in the past, I was not shocked.

Since childhood I have been blessed with an unusual ability to receive certain vibrations from people of spiritual significance, and the warm sensation that I got from touching Zeola's hand was a good example. We connected almost instantly. I felt very comfortable in her presence and I later found out that she felt the same.

As soon as I locked the car doors and turned on the key and waited for her to secure her seat belt I headed for Hollywood. By the time I got to Olympic Blvd. I remembered that someone in the production office had mentioned that Zeola liked a particular pasta place in West Los Angeles, so I

5

turned left and proceeded to West LA, and it worked out well. The food was good, and our conversation flowed smoothly. However, all the while we were eating and talking, I could see an almost eerie resemblance of Marvin in her smile. It was almost as if someone had placed a transparent photograph of Marvin over her face, and every once in a while I could see a vision of Marvin in place of Zeola.

A couple of times during lunch I had to re-adjust my thinking in order to focus on what she was saying because I kept feeling the presence of a third party at our table, and it was driving me crazy. But of course nobody was there but the two of us. I convinced myself that my imagination was running away with me because Zeola looked so much like Marvin.

Finally, I put it all out of my mind and focused on a nice afternoon with a very nice lady. All the while, the image of Marvin's face over Zeola's was stored in the back of my mind because the incident seemed so real. I knew that something had happened that day, I just couldn't figure out what it was. Approximately one month later it all came through loud and clear.

CHAPTER
2

THE SHOOTING

This was my first writing session with Zeola, so I wanted everything to be comfortable for her. I remembered the pleasant time that we had at the restaurant and knew that I could make a pretty good pasta dish myself so I decided to prepare a linguini salad with red bell peppers, garlic, tomatoes and my special pesto sauce and shrimp. While I was chopping the garlic and washing the fresh tomatoes I began wondering what the day was going to be like with Zeola.

I knew that this was going to be a difficult one because our goal was to discuss what happened the day of the shooting. So, after we finished our lunch and I cleared the table and we relaxed for a few minutes with a glass of merlot wine, I turned on the tape recorder, grabbed my pen and tablet as Zeola proceeded to share with me her innermost thoughts about Marvin's ill-timely death.

"Nobody was good enough for me until Marvin met my new boyfriend, Gary, who was such a man's man that there was really nothing negative Marvin could say about him. Gary wasn't afraid of anything or anybody. Marvin really liked him so we got married and Marvin started using Gary as his driver as well as his security guard. Gary also ran Marvin's errands and things."

A few days before the shooting Zeola recalled Marvin summoning Gary to the big house and instructing him to collect all the guns in the house and have them cleaned. She said that there were about five of them.

"I don't know if the guns were licensed or not, but Father said he had them because the house was so big, and he felt that he needed protection."

Zeola said that Gary called her father 'Pop'. *"He was the only person to call him that."* She said that she remembered Gary telling her that he went to her father and said, *"Pop,*

Marvin wants me to take all the guns to have them cleaned." Zeola said that her father gave Gary all of the guns except one. *"He said he wanted to keep one gun for protection,"* she explained. Zeola was very adamant when she said that Marvin could have insisted that all of the guns leave the house, but he didn't. She emphasized the fact that Marvin allowed her father to keep one of them. I asked her what she meant by that statement because in my mind I could see why Gay Sr. would want to keep one of the guns for protection. And I could see why Marvin allowed it, but Zeola felt differently.

She replied, *"If Marvin had insisted, Father would have been forced to give Gary the gun, but Marvin didn't insist. Gary told me that he had asked Marvin about the last gun twice and Marvin told him to leave it. So Gary brought the guns to our house."*

That still did not answer my question, but she was so sure that her statement made sense that I left it alone for a while. Later, I understood her to mean that she believes that Marvin left the gun there so that his father could kill him. This remained unclear until several sessions later. And when I did 'get it' I didn't necessarily agree with her.

The analogy that Marvin left one gun versus five guns for the sole purpose of his father killing him seemed a bit bizarre to me. I kept asking myself what was the difference in having one gun or five. If he wanted to make sure that his father succeeded, why not keep all of the guns? But since Zeola was so adamant about her reasoning I said nothing else, and we move on.

The night before the shooting Zeola said that Gary was with Marvin. Gary told her that Marvin asked him to come back to the big house at 5:30 the next morning to take him to the beach so that he could meditate and pray during sunrise. Unfortunately, on Gary's way home that night the police stopped him because the truck that he was driving had no tags, so he was taken to jail. Zeola said that Gary told her to contact Marvin who got his ex-manager named Marilyn to post bail.

Once again thoughts raced through my head. Could Marvin have wanted to go to the beach that morning to pray before dying? That was a possibility, but according to Zeola he visited the beach for prayer quite often, therefore his request was not out of the ordinary.

When Zeola picked Gary up the next morning she said that they stopped to get a sandwich on Fairfax and Olympic and then went home. By 9:00 a.m. Zeola said that they were both in bed eating their sandwiches while Gary told her about his whole experience in jail.

"Around 11:00 a.m. April 1, 1984 I got a phone call from Frankie's wife, Irene, telling me that our father had just shot Marvin and that I should come right away."

Being that it was April Fools Day, and Zeola and Frankie always played jokes on each other, Zeola said that she remembered being annoyed with Irene for telling her that her father had just shot Marvin. Zeola said that she told Irene that she didn't think that her joke was very funny, but the stress in Irene's voice, plus, the fact that Irene seldom called her by her nickname made her realize that Irene wasn't joking.

"Sweetsie, you need to come up here right now. Father really did shoot Marvin."

Zeola said that Frankie lived in a three-bedroom apartment over the six-car garage at the back of the big house so he was able to get to the house right after the shooting occurred, but she and her husband, Gary, lived further away.

"When I told Gary that Father had just shot Marvin, I was angry and upset, but I wasn't thinking that he had killed him. I

thought maybe he had shot him in the leg or something. But even so, it was still a serious matter so Gary grabbed only his wallet, and I went as I was, and we rushed out of the house immediately."

Zeola said that it would normally take about 9 minutes to get from where she and Gary lived in West Los Angeles to the big house on Gramercy Place, but this time she said that Gary out-did himself.

"If there was a traffic law to be broken, Gary broke it that day." She said that Gary drove through every red light and ignored all of the stop signs.

"He broke every traffic law in the book, other than to hit a pedestrian."

According to Zeola, they arrived at the house in a little less than three minutes after the phone call.

By now Zeola had cleaned out her roach clip, and put her paraphernalia on the table and was talking incessantly.

"Our adrenalin was going crazy. When we got there we saw Father sitting outside on the wooden bench, so Gary rushed past him and ran up the stairs to see what he could do to help. I walked up to Father and asked him why he shot Marvin. Looking dazed, all that he said was, "I had to. I had to." So I just shook my head in disgust and hurried into the house. I still didn't know how bad it was. And I would have never dreamed in a million years that my brother was dead."

The moment she entered the foyer of the big eight bedroom Tudor-style house she hesitated because an unusual dead silence had filled the downstairs. She said that it sent chills down her spine. And for that brief moment she could not move. She remembered looking to her left into the well-maintained music room and then to her right, which was the playroom. Still, she could not move forward. Instead, she continued to assess the downstairs from the vestibule. Finally, far back in the corner of the playroom Zeola said that she spotted her mother slowly rocking back and forth in her old rocking chair.

"*She looked so pitifully frightened.*" Zeola sadly recalled. She said that she rushed over to her mother and asked her what had happened and Alberta said that 'Doc' had shot Marvin and that she knew that Marvin was dead.

"*All that I could do at that moment was fall to my knees and lay my head in her lap and cry.*"

Zeola said that her mother was trembling uncontrollably. She said that Alberta told her that she was scared and worried. She said that her mother thought that 'Doc' was going to kill her too.

I was grateful when it became obvious that Zeola was going to be very candid with her thoughts and feelings about Marvin and her father because I wanted answers to all the questions that I had asked myself on the day of the funeral.

I felt good knowing that we had connected both mentally and spiritually. I use the word spiritual because I believe that everything happens for a reason, and there are no accidents. And the fact that I ended up writing this story about this wonderful man must have happened for a reason, and I was determined to do the best I could to tell her story the way she wanted it to be told.

It was soon after that the paramedics pulled up outside. Gary and Frankie were upstairs with Marvin's body when Zeola said that she suddenly remembered that a bag of crack cocaine was up there in the drawer by Marvin's bed, and she didn't want the police to come in and find it. Still unable to go up those stairs and see her brother shot and hurt, Zeola remembered yelling to Gary to hide the drugs. She said that she wasn't too concerned about any powdered cocaine that might have been left around because it didn't mean the same in those days. It was common knowledge that entertainers used powdered cocaine as a recreational drug, but the media would have had a field day talking about Marvin having an addiction to crack.

"Especially, knowing that Marvin wasn't even using crack at that time." Zeola insisted.

Suddenly something did not feel right to me because I had previously read that the autopsy indicated that Marvin was, in fact, on drugs. It stated that Marvin had both cocaine and angel dust in his system.

I wanted so badly to say to Zeola that that was not what I read in the newspaper, but she was a little too out of sorts for me to interject such a negative comment at that time. I felt that it just would not have been appropriate. I figured that it would probably play itself out at a later date, and it did.

Zeola must have noticed the expression on my face because she quickly clarified her statement by explaining to me that the crack cocaine that was in Marvin's drawer had been there for several months. She further explained that Marvin left it there as sort of a test of strength for himself. Afterward I thought about what I had read and remembered that the article mentioned cocaine and angel dust but made no reference to crack. So maybe Zeola was partially correct. He was doing drugs, but he was not on crack. Unfortunately, I can't ask her about it now that we aren't communicating.

"When the paramedics came, I thought it was strange that they went upstairs without a gurney."

Zeola said that she was sitting with her mother when the paramedics arrived. She described how that the two of them were both hugging each other and watching from the playroom.

"I just couldn't understand why they didn't take that gurney up those steps." Zeola repeated.

"Maw finally stopped crying for a brief moment while the paramedics were upstairs. But she was still frightened and nervous."

About five or ten minutes later Gary and Frankie came down the stairs carrying Marvin's body. When Zeola first realized that they were bringing him downstairs she said that she couldn't look. And finally, when she did look up she noticed that Gary had hold of the top part of Marvin's body and Frankie had the bottom, and they placed him on the gurney.

"The moment I saw the middle part of Marvin's body so limp, my heart sank. And even though Ma kept insisting that Marvin was dead, I kept insisting that he was not."

Zeola remembered the paramedics lifting Marvin's arms and placing them over his stomach and then covering him up. By then she said that she was so busy comforting her mother and crying so uncontrollably, that she couldn't remember whether or not they covered Marvin's face before they took him out of the house. She just remembers the dead silence that permeated the Gay's old mansion.

The paramedics took Marvin's body out of the house and placed him in the ambulance and quietly drove off with no flashing lights and no blaring sirens. Gary and Zeola, who were still in denial, followed the ambulance wondering why the sirens were not blaring.

All the way to the hospital Zeola said that she prayed, *"God, please don't let him die."* But it was too late. Marvin was dead on arrival at the hospital.

"Marvin finally got his peace of mind." Zeola whispered. *"He wanted to die. He was so unhappy. He had to deal with the promoters, the black mafia, the voices, my mom's illness and my*

14

father's despicable jealousies. And about a week or so before his death I saw a telegram that he had gotten from Jan, his ex-wife, telling him that he would never see his kids again as long as he lived. Little did she know how true that statement was because he never did see his kids again."

There was a brief moment of silence between the two of us after that last comment about Marvin not ever seeing his children again. I was making notes, and Zeola was solemnly smoking a joint. What could be said at that point? All I could think of was how terribly sad it must have been for this troubled and lonely man during that time. It is so hard to believe that there wasn't one single solitary person who could truly help him through those dark times. It's equally hard to imagine what his feelings of loneliness and despair must have been like.

Almost immediately, I knew that this book was going to be a roller coaster ride for me because Zeola and I had been talking less than an hour and already I felt anxieties rising from the pit of my stomach.

It was difficult listening to her because I could see the uneasiness in her facial expressions, which created a bit of anxiety in me. I began to imagine how awful it must have felt racing through the streets of Los Angeles not knowing exactly what to expect upon arrival. I remember feeling almost as badly as I did the day I heard it on the television back in 1984. It felt as if it had just happened the day before. I think that we both had watery eyes, so I turned off the tape recorder and offered her another glass of wine just to interrupt the sadness that we both were feeling. I was thinking, *"Maybe you don't need a break this quick, but I do."* So we took time out to sip the wine and breathe. After that I got up and walked out on to my patio and just stood there for a moment.

The afternoon sun had turned a bright reddish-orange and was about to set in the west out beyond Venice Beach. For a brief moment all I could do was thank God for allowing me to be in that very spot at that very moment to witness that beautiful crimson sky because it took my mind off the things that Zeola had just talked about. I thought to myself that I had only just started listening to this incredible story and already I knew that I was ever so grateful not to be a member of the Gay household.

Zeola waited patiently on the sofa until I returned to my favorite cushiony side chair facing diagonally to her. When I sat down and looked over at her I could tell that she was anxious to finish her story because she immediately started talking.

She remembered Marvin telling her numerous times how much he needed some peace in his life.

"Marvin told me how much he would love to be at peace with God. Keep in mind he wasn't doing drugs at this time. He wasn't doing anything except sitting around the house with Maw in his old blue robe and brown straw hat and reading the bible. Or, he would sit in the window looking out over the freeway like Father did, except Marvin would be sitting there talking to Maw or me about suicide."

Zeola said that Marvin had been talking about his death for some time. She believes that he started planning his death the minute he found out that Alberta had cancer.

"I can't emphasize enough how many times Marvin said that he did not want to be around when she dies."

This was almost unimaginable that someone who was so loved and admired by so many millions of people felt that he had nobody to turn to except her mother. It was obvious that Alberta was Marvin's only saving grace. The fact that the one person who had his back 'unconditionally' was about to leave him forever must have been devastating for him.

One can only imagine the pain he must have suffered.

CHAPTER
3

FAMILY

The Gay kids were born and raised in the projects in Washington DC. *"We were not permitted to go outside and play with other kids because we were Pentecostal,"* Zeola said. So they made up their own games and played inside the house.

"I remember when Marvin and Jean would put me on a blanket from our bed and throw me up in the air and catch me. When I think about it now, I must have been out of my mind allowing them to do that to me. But it was fun. They never dropped me. And Frankie would join us when we put the blanket on the stairs and all of us would get on it and slide down the steps together like a little train. There wasn't a lot of fun in our house, so we created our own," Zeola recalled, as she crossed her legs, and puffed on her newly rolled joint.

"My family was always very hair conscious. And my father did wear a lot of wigs, and some of them were sort of tacky. And when he didn't wear wigs, he would have Maw press and curl his hair. And I guess that made him look a little feminine too. Maybe we were all like this because my mom had beautiful hair, and we all wished that our hair looked like hers. When she would wash it we all would admire how it would turn into big curly locks. My mom was really beautiful, and nobody had hair like hers. Nobody. And it was probably best for me because I already knew how cute I was. I had really nice legs. I was shapely and small. All I needed was the hair. But if I had had the hair, I probably wouldn't have had a friend in the world. They probably wouldn't have been able to tolerate me. I'm just honest about the whole thing. I looked good and I knew it. I think Father felt the same way. I think that he believed that the wigs and soft things looked good on him and possibly helped enhance his sensuality."

In addition to the supposedly freakiness and enhanced sensuality, the Gay family has another very distinguishable trait, according to Zeola. She said that when they get excited or argue their voices automatically get higher and higher, and become very loud.

"So we could hear Marvin and my father when they argued no matter where they were in the house. "

She said that even though Frankie spoke with a very soft tone, when he got angry it was the total opposite.

"When I lived with my sister, Jeanne, and she and her son's father would argue, I would cringe because it would take me back to Father. I would get so scared and nervous and my heart would beat real fast because she was just as devastating in her arguments as Father, Marvin and Frankie, and probably as I am."

Zeola said that after they became adults they knew just how far to take a disagreement with Gay Sr. She said that as long as they remained respectful they could say whatever they wanted. But when things got to that point where it was getting out of hand, they knew to stop when it got to that line of disrespect. "But Marvin ignored that line." She said that he would go however far he needed to go to get his point across. He was Marvin.

So, now Zeola says that when she argues she hears her mom's voice in her head telling her to 'bend.' She said that she used to think to herself, *"Damn, how many times do I have to bend? My back is fucking breaking."*

But now Zeola said that she realizes that if she hadn't bent, it would have kept going on and on and on. Now, she says that she understands what her mother's reasoning was about and she has gotten to a point where she doesn't even mind bending.

"I guess it comes with age. If I have to be the one to make the first step and apologize, I think to myself, 'Whatever.'"

Zeola said that whenever Marvin and her father's arguments on the telephone would escalate, Gay Sr. was generally the first to hang up because Marvin would generally resort to cussing, and Gay Sr. couldn't handle that. She said that in that day and age, when you cussed it seemed like you were winning, so Gay Sr. would hang up. But then Zeola said that that would cause another problem.

"Father would then carry the argument over to our mother. So Maw would ask Marvin not to harass his father for her sake. And that was the last thing Marvin would want. But don't think that I am saying that Maw couldn't hold her own. She wasn't a pushover. She would speak her mind. But she was more about peace."

Zeola said that if her mother thought that being silent was the best way to go then she would be silent. She often said, *"Who can argue with silence? Just because I'm not saying anything doesn't mean that you're right. It just means that I am finished dealing with the issue."*

I can clearly understand why the Gay children admired and loved their mother so much. Even though she seemed like the Rock of Gibraltar, I am sure that she had her moments of weakness and despair especially when dealing with Gay Sr..

I told Zeola that it seemed obvious to me that she and Jeanne and Frankie had inherited a bit of their parents' melodious talents because Zeola had said that they all sang in church.

"But Marvin was blessed with all of it and more." Zeola commented.

"I was told many times by my mother that even when Marvin was three and four years old he would set the church on fire with his singing. I wish I could have seen him. It must have been so awesome watching him perform at that young age."

By the time Zeola was old enough to sing in the children's choir she said that Marvin was doing professional solos in the church.

"When Marvin finished bringing the congregation to its feet with his singing there wasn't much left for Father to do, and he wasn't happy about it at all because the members seemed like they were all ready to go home after Marvin's solos ended."

The church consisted of a small group of church folks, but Zeola said she remembers them making a lot of noise. She said that they had a real good time in those days. *"Especially, when Marvin sang."*

Zeola said that it was obvious to most of the family as well as some of the church members that Gay Sr. resented his son's talent even though Marvin Jr. was just a little kid. *"But Marvin didn't care. Once the spirit hit him and he had the church jumping and clapping and shouting, there was no stopping him."*

Zeola recalled that even her father's stern frowns of disapproval and sometimes brief interjections such as *"Praise the Lord, but let's move on now."* never seemed to affect Marvin. She said that he just kept going and going, like the little battery-charged bunny rabbit in the television commercials, and the congregation went right along with him until they were all exhausted from the good old-fashioned Pentecostal spirit.

"I think that maybe some of the whippings that Marvin received after church services were because of his lengthy recitals. But I can't be sure."

Zeola fumbled with her fingers in a nervous-like manner. It seemed as though she just didn't like finding fault with her father even though she knew deep down inside that he deserved it. She obviously had a bit of kindness in a little corner of her heart for him despite all that he had done. And the use of marijuana seemed to help her cope.

I had read somewhere that she had told a writer that her father was a good man, and that he really loved Marvin and was not jealous of him, so I asked her about it. She said that the person interviewing her made her feel uncomfortable about telling the truth. She said that the lady convinced her that she shouldn't talk about anything negative. So Zeola said that she's lied to people for all these years. She told me that I made her feel comfortable in telling the truth. I thanked her and even though we moved on, I could still tell that she was holding back on the complete truth about how ruthless and arrogant Gay Sr. really was.

"Other than the church stuff with Marvin, I can't think of any other time that we got a beating for absolutely nothing. No, Father didn't just wake up in the morning and say 'I think I'll beat the kids today.' It wasn't like that. And he would always be fair. He would always give us a chance to talk. He would say something like 'Didn't I tell you not to go next door and play?' And if we did go next door, that called for a spanking. So we all knew that about Father. Marvin knew it too, but he continued to challenge him."

Although I understood what Zeola meant, I still had a hard time dealing with their father's ideas for raising children. Some things still did not set well with me. She still seemed to be defending him in some small way. I only justified her actions by the fact that he is still her father in spite of himself.

Zeola said that she, Marvin and Frankie had made a pact amongst them never to tell on each other. They decided that they would do whatever it took to keep Father from beating them.

"Depending on his mood, we could all end up getting whipped with that thick leather belt of his."

Once again, her statement bothered me. She had just told me that every beating that they got was for a good reason, and now she was telling me that their beatings depended on Gay Sr.'s moods. *"She is still her father's child,"* I thought.

Zeola said that Marvin always kept his word with Frankie and her.

"He never told on us, and we never told on him."

I quickly noticed that Zeola had not mentioned her sister, so I asked why she didn't include Jeanne, and she paused a moment without responding. So I asked her again, and this time she became visibly agitated, and immediately reached for her roach clip, which still contained a small amount of weed. She lit it and then held it in and waited a moment until she felt that it had done whatever she needed it to do, and then she responded. She said that it was not a mistake that she left her sister out of the group. She stated that her sister would tell on all of them.

"Jeanne was a tattle tale. Anything we did that was against the rules, she would tell it. She acted like it was her obligation to tell on everybody. I never understood that. She was always different from the rest of us. But I think she loved us, and I know that we loved her."

Zeola continued to explain the situation between Jeanne and the others.

"I used to wonder if it was because she was the only one of us who looked like our father that maybe she thought a little bit like him, but I was just a little kid and didn't know how to analyze things. I love my sister and I know that she loves me despite our childhood differences."

Our session was about to come to an end, so Zeola finished the weed in her clip, dumped the ashes in my trash can and carefully wiped out my ash tray and placed it back on the table. She then proceeded to put her paraphernalia away in her big black bag and continued to reflect on the past.

She said that she remembered once when she was seven years old and Marvin was a teenager, her father did something unusual.

"He went to work." We both laughed at that statement.

When Gay Sr. left for work that day Zeola said that he told the kids not to open the door for anybody. He said that they could have absolutely no company whatsoever.

"He also said that we were not to play ball in the house. But being kids we didn't listen. I guess we felt the freedom of Father's absence, so Frankie and I decided to play ball, and I threw the ball to Frankie and he missed it and the ball hit a porcelain black panther that belonged to my father. I think everybody had one in those days. Well, the ball broke the panther and I started crying because I knew I was going to get a whipping. I cried and I cried, and Marvin came over to me and held me and told me not to cry. He said that he would take the blame for it. He said that he would tell Father that he broke it. Man, I couldn't believe it. I thought that was the greatest thing I had ever known. I said to myself, 'Boy, I really love him!'"

When Father came home Zeola said that Marvin did take the blame, and her father didn't beat him because he confessed. Zeola said that she remembered thinking, *"God sure stepped in this time. He saved Marvin from getting a beating because Marvin saved me from getting one."*

Zeola really enjoyed talking about Marvin and Frankie, but when she talked about Jeanne, it seemed to be on a different level. The love was obviously there, but the joy was not.

"If that had happened with my sister Jeanne, I know that she would not have taken the fall for me. She just wasn't like that. Jeanne would have told Father that I did it out of fear of her getting a beating for lying."

25

Zeola insisted that her mother was not weak despite her father.

"Maw just never stopped trying to keep the peace. She would try her best to make sure that nobody put their father in a bad mood because he would fuss at everybody. She would say, 'Make sure you go up there and speak to your father.'"

Zeola said that her mother made sure that everybody stayed in school and didn't get into any serious trouble. She told me that Jean, Marvin and Frankie were smart like their father, and although none of them went to a university, all three of them were 'A' students.

At that moment I once again became impressed with Alberta because it must have taken a lot for this woman to maintain this household, work long hours, take care of four children and still be able to tolerate the abrasiveness of this man. I realize that back-in-the-day women were a bit more submissive than they are today, but this was just beyond anything that I could imagine. All that I can say is that something was working right if the children were doing well in school, and seemed to be of good spirit.

Zeola said she was only a 'B-C' student yet she was the one who got the chance to go to junior college. According to her, that's about as far as anybody in her family ever got in school.

"In those days college wasn't a big deal in our neighborhood unless you wanted to be something special. And even though Jean expressed that desire, she ended up joining the Civil Air Force Patrol and marrying some guy in the air force. Frankie was just Frankie, and Marvin, continued to do his own thing."

After school Zeola said that Marvin was always the one that everybody would end up looking for.

"He seldom came straight home from school." Zeola chuckled. *"Sometimes he would sneak in late at night and Jeanne would threaten to tell on him, and they would get into fights. They used to fight a lot. Jeanne would always win when it was a physical fight, but Marvin always won if it dealt with mental issues. He loved the mind games, but he never played them on Frankie and me."*

Zeola said that Marvin only messed with Jeanne because she would sometimes get them all in trouble.

"We feared Father so much when we were little, but we loved him too."

This was a good day so far. We had had a good time laughing and reminiscing about Zeola's past with Marvin and her seemingly dysfunctional family. It was just so hard for me to believe that Gay Sr. had been a minister at one time, wearing all those wigs and soft things. Maybe this all started after his ministry days were over. Unfortunately, I can't ask Zeola about it.

Zeola told me how they had to say 'Good morning, Father" and "Good night, Father", even if he was angry and would not respond.

"He was real strict like that." She said defensively.

She said that she was afraid to bring playmates to the house because if Gay Sr. found out that their friends had come in and not made that extra effort to locate and acknowledge him, he would put them out of the house once he realized that they were there.

"Marvin was the only one of us kids whose spirit had not been broken by Father's threats. Marvin brought his friends home anyway, and didn't force them to do any of Father's demands. He just kept them away from him. Marvin continued to beat to a different drum than the rest of us. I figure that he probably knew

27

Audrey King Lewis

that his voice would be his ticket out of the house and away from Father."

I quickly noticed a look on Zeola's face after making that statement. It seemed as if she were 'wishing that she had had a way out.' But I didn't pursue the moment.

CHAPTER
4

FATHER

Although Zeola had described herself to me on numerous occasions as the baby of the family and the apple of everybody's eye while growing up, there still remained a great deal of emptiness and pain in her voice when she talked about some of the family members, especially her father.

"My father was a disciplinarian." She explained. *"He wasn't really a 'daddy.' He never played with us or hugged us or did the things that I saw other kid's fathers doing. To be honest, I don't really think I know what a 'daddy' is. But I do know that my father wasn't one of them."*

Whenever Zeola talked about her father her voice became small and sometimes shaky as she squirmed in her seat like a little girl reliving childhood moments of discipline from daddy.

"He always demanded that we call him 'Father'." She began. *"He kept order and made sure that we kept the house clean, watched our manners and obeyed him by saying 'yes sir' and 'no sir.' We weren't allowed to say, 'huh?' or 'What you say?' We were raised to respect our elders and not to talk back. We were told as kids that we should stay in our place. When company would come to the house, we would speak to them and then go to our quarters. Those were Father's orders."* Zeola ended this statement by tucking her head as if somebody had just told her to go to her room. Her childlike qualities such as her soft and pleasant voice along with her sometimes very sweet mannerisms were always interesting to me. One minute she was this gentle little creature who was the sweet and lovely baby sister of Marvin, Jeanne and Frankie and the next minute the word, 'mother-fucker' would flow from her lips like a well seasoned long shore man.

When I asked her what the general atmosphere was like in their house during breakfast or dinner, she lowered her head once again but this time it wasn't one of her girlish moves. She was looking for something, and she quickly found it. Lying on the coffee table beside her purse was a marijuana joint. She reached for it and then proceeded to answer my question.

"Father seldom ate with the rest of us," she admitted quite candidly. And then she flicked her red Bic cigarette lighter and placed the joint to her lips and slowly inhaled. After holding the smoke a moment she gradually let it out through her mouth. I could tell by the look of satisfaction on her face that she not only had been doing this a very long time, but that she also enjoyed every bit of it. But please let me clarify something. I am not by any means trying to describe her as some junkie with a needle. That is not what I mean at all. I truly think that Zeola just enjoys smoking weed, like most marijuana users. The weed never seemed to change her personality or allow her to go to sleep. It was just 'pot'. It seemed to do what it does for most people. It relaxed her.

I don't know why I didn't get contact high whenever we got together, but the smoke never seemed to affect me. I guess I was so intent on listening to her every word that I just wasn't open to it. Or, maybe I had been affected and didn't realize it. But I think that if I had been inhaling the least bit of her smoke I would have been able to tell. Wouldn't that be a sorry sight? Both of us leaning back on the sofa relaxed and traveling down memory lane with nobody taking notes of anything that was being said and no tape recorder rolling. No, I don't think the weed affected me at all. I think that keeping my patio door open and generally sitting near the opened doorway took care of that. And my tape recorder was like my third arm. We never started talking without recording every word.

Finally, after a couple of hits, Zeola began to speak more freely about the family meals.

"Most of the time, Maw would take his food tray upstairs to his bedroom. But there were times when he was in such an ugly mood that even she was not permitted to enter."

Zeola said that whenever this would happen her mother would have one of the kids take a plate up to him. And when it was Zeola's turn to carry the tray to his room she recalled being so scared that she could barely make it up the steps. She remembers her little hands shaking almost to the point of dropping the tray, which was filled with her mother's best china. She would stand at the bottom of the long wooden staircase and wonder if she would ever make it to the top. And once she would get there, she said that she would walk slowly down the hall and approach her father's door cautiously. She remembers hoping with all her might that he would not respond to her knock. Sometimes she said that she would barely tap on the door hoping that he wouldn't hear it so that she could go back downstairs and tell her mother that he didn't answer. But that never worked. He always responded, and it was generally that same, thunderous and intimidating voice.

"Who is it? What? Why are you knocking on my door?"

"Father, here's your food."

"Well, leave it at the door!"

Relieved when he did not come out, she said that she would gently place the tray filled with the beautifully decorated dishes and shiny flatware in the hallway on the freshly waxed hardwood floor in front of his door, careful not to make too much noise with the tray. Zeola said that there were times when she would go to bed and she would see her father's meal still sitting in the hallway outside his door.

"Things always had to be Father's way. He would set the tone in the house. And I think drinking might have had a lot to do with

whatever the tone would be for that day. I didn't realize that my father drank heavily because he never seemed drunk. He just fussed at our mother a lot. It wasn't until I was old enough to recognize the Vodka bottles that I realized that he had a drinking problem."

I think Zeola must have read my face when she was telling me this because I couldn't believe what I was hearing. To me, this man sounded like a fictional character from an old horror movie. But this was her father, and I respected what she had to say, so I continued to listen. And to be honest, I found myself anxiously waiting to hear more about this seemingly self-centered and obnoxious individual. Up until now, I had had a hard time envisioning this man killing his own son. But now I was beginning to see why his mind allowed himself to do what he did, and at the same time I was beginning to understand Zeola's attraction to his dominance.

"It is so important to me to tell the world that even though my father was a very complicated and domineering man, he did love all of us, including Marvin, but he loved us in his own way."

I thought to myself, *"Yeah, right. If that is love, I don't need it."*

Still trying to convince me that this strange individual was not a monster, Zeola began boasting about her father being a well-read authority figure. She said that he was extremely articulate, and that he dominated most conversations amongst his peers.

"Nobody got a word in when Father was speaking at the church. And if he was interrupted, he showed his displeasure, especially when Marvin Jr. would take too long singing."

She demonstrated how Gay Sr. would strut up and down the pulpit area obviously annoyed at Marvin who had all the church members on their feet shouting and clapping.

33

All during the while Zeola was imitating her father I was trying to find the correct moment to ask her about the rumors that her father was gay. I had hoped that this would not taint our working relationship, but the question needed to be addressed. So I waited until she lit up another joint, and seemed to be in a very mellow mood before I approached the subject. And to my surprise, she opened up without hesitation.

Zeola admitted that there was a bit of delicateness about her father, but she insisted that he was not gay. And in defense of him, she contended that her brother, Marvin, had similar qualities.

"That's what made Marvin so sensuous. He was never afraid to get in touch with his sensitive side. To me, that has absolutely nothing to do with being gay because I know for a fact that both Marvin Jr. and my father loved women."

Zeola confessed to me that her father did like to wear soft things. She thinks that this is what confused a lot of people.

"Father liked cashmere and he loved silks and satins. But most of his silks and satins were dinner jackets and silk pajamas. There have always been rumors about the possibility of my father being gay, but it wasn't true," Zeola insisted.

She remains convinced that her father loved only women. She said that when they lived in the projects back in the 50's her father fooled around with the lady who took care of them while her mother was at work.

"I can't remember whether it was my sister or one of my brothers who caught them in bed together. I haven't forgotten that her name was Bea. I remember not liking her after that because she made my mom think that she was her best friend."

Zeola also said that she remembers seeing her father 'screw around' with another lady in the back alley behind the projects.

"I didn't know her name, but I knew what they were doing. I knew that my father shouldn't have been kissing and hugging her the way that he was. Everybody knew about them. Father screwed most of the women that came to our house, so I know he liked to fuck women."

I tried to get a general description of those women from Zeola, but she said that she was such a little girl when those things went on that she wasn't able to remember many details. She just remembers that they were all good-looking and tall. Well, tall wasn't a good description I thought because even now Zeola can't be much more than about 5'2" as an adult, so one can only imagine how tall these ladies must have looked to a small child.

Now that I had realized that Zeola is so forthcoming with information about her father I decided to dig deeper into the life of the infamous Gay Sr., and she willingly went along for the ride.

For some reason this session seemed like it was a good form of therapy for Zeola. I'm not a shrink, but I do know when somebody's attitude starts to change, and she was definitely changing. She seemed as anxious to talk about this as I was to listen.

"My parents told me that they met at a Pentecostal church in Kentucky. Maw was just getting into the Pentecostal religion and was visiting the church where Father was speaking. She said that she was at the church because she liked another minister who was Father's rival."

Zeola talked openly. She said that the two men were both Bishops and in competition with each other to become the head apostle for the Pentecostal churches all over the world. She said that the minister's name was Bishop Rollins.

"I don't know where he is today," She commented.

Both Bishops lived in Kentucky, so Zeola said that her father decided to move to Washington DC, not realizing that there weren't very many Pentecostal members there.

"Father soon found himself stuck with a small storefront church consisting of only two families, while the other Bishop became wealthy because he stayed in Kentucky where the Pentecostal churches were full of members."

Zeola seemed convinced that this was part of what contributed to her father's heavy drinking and unpredictable mood swings. Not to mention the fact that Little Marvin Jr. had now practically stolen the storefront congregation away from Gay Sr. with his singing talents.

"Father was tall and thin with high cheekbones and copper toned skin. He had a very striking appearance, and he knew how to demand attention. Sometimes he might raise his voice a little, but he never yelled at anybody because he didn't have to. His voice projected in such a way that whenever he spoke everybody listened. Everybody, that is, except Marvin. Marvin is the only person that I know who had the courage to challenge Father."

Zeola went on to say that Marvin always took chances with their father. Most of the time, she said that their father would beat them naked, but sometimes if Marvin knew that he was going to get a quick whipping with his clothes on, he would rush upstairs and stuff his pants with towels and wash cloths in order to pad his butt.

"I would always tell him that he's going to get caught and it was going to be worse. But the strange thing was that Father would see the padding and wouldn't say anything. I knew he could see it because I could see it. I guess he figured that if Marvin had enough courage to do that, then he would just let it slide. Marvin and Father were so much alike when it came to the mind games that I think Father sort of respected Marvin for his efforts."

36

What amazed me most was when Zeola said that she truly believed that their father generally beat them naked for good reasons.

Once again I spoke up in disgust, which I knew was not appropriate, but I could not keep my silence any longer. All that I envisioned while she was describing the beatings were these precious little children spread out on their beds like a bunch of slaves being whipped by their master, and that was about to drive me crazy. I told Zeola that it was not possible for somebody to be that cruel. She said that she didn't feel that it was about being cruel. She said that it was about respect. She seemed convinced that they deserved what they usually got from him, especially if they lied about something. She said that he could not stand a liar. I wanted so badly to say how much I could not stand her father, but this time I zipped my lip and we continued.

"I remember the time Father followed me home after school." She began. *"He had told me to come straight home, and I didn't. He had repeatedly said to me not to stop. He said, 'Just come straight home.' In those days we walked to and from school, and our junior high school was far away. But for some reason that day I took my time coming home. I remember deliberately scraping my shoes on the sidewalk because I hated those oxford shoes that we got from the thrift shop. I would scrape them everyday, trying to wear them out. I also remember looking over the fence and playing with this little dog, and then I walked along a brick walkway the rest of the way. Anyway, I ended up a little late getting home, and when Father asked me why I was late, I told him that I didn't know. And I really did not know why I was late. To me, I did come right home. But Father said, 'I am going to ask you one more time why you are late coming home.'"*

By this time Zeola said that she was getting really scared, and her heart was beating fast because her father continued to interrogate her.

"So you didn't stop off and play with the little dog?" He asked.

Well, before Zeola could think she said, "No Sir." She said that she remembered being really scared at that moment because she knew that he wasn't finished with her.

"You didn't stop and pick some flowers?"

Zeola contended that if she had used a little common sense that she would have been able to figure out that he had followed her, but fear took over and she handled it all wrong. She lied again.

"Father said that I should go upstairs and prepare for my whipping. He said he was not going to beat me because I was late, but because I lied to him."

Zeola said that when he told her to go upstairs that it meant that she was going to be whipped naked, so she proceeded up the stairs with quiet tears rolling down her cheeks. She said that she hated the thought of getting naked for him more than the beating that she was about to receive.

At that moment I stopped taking notes and looked up at Zeola because her voice had suddenly changed. The expression on her face reminded me of a sad little girl reliving a bad incident in her past. This struck me strange. Why did she hate the part about getting naked in front of her father more than the beating? She was a little girl, and this was her father. For a brief moment it sounded as if she was leaving something out about the nakedness, and I started to ask her about it, but she had already moved on with her story so I held that question for later.

Zeola went on to explain that her father didn't believe in chasing them around the room because he said that he might hit one of them in the wrong place, so in preparation for their beatings, they were required to lay naked on their stomachs with their hands placed firmly on the head board of the bed, and they were absolutely not allowed to squirm, kick or scream and cry as he beat them with his thick leather belt across their bare buttocks.

"So I went upstairs and took off all of my clothes and then I laid naked on top of the bed waiting tearfully for my beating. I clearly remember this particular incident because I was just beginning to blossom into a young woman, and I didn't like for anybody to see me naked, especially my father."

Now the despair in her voice was making more sense. The thought of having to lay on a bed naked and wait for some jackass to come along and beat on me like an old dirty rug was unimaginable to me, especially for stopping to pick a few flowers or pausing to pet a little dog.

Zeola remembered that there were seventeen steps for her father to climb to get to her. She still recalled counting them as he approached the top of the stairs.

"I will never forget them because Father took them that day one step at a time as if he was taunting me."

And that monster succeeded because she said by the time he reached the top of the stairs she was a complete basket case. She said that she doesn't remember what the temperature was in her bedroom, but she does remember sweating and shivering at the same time. She remembered that she had perspired so much in those few minutes that the sheets began to stick to her little body.

Jeanne and Zeola's room was at the top of the stairs, and their father's room was next door. She remembered her father coming up the stairs and walking slowly past her room and then entering his room and closing the door. She remembered hearing him in there jingling the belts. She said that he was probably trying to choose the right one to use. After about three or four minutes the jingling stopped and Gay Sr. came out of his room and slowly closed his door and came back toward her room. But, when he got to her door, Zeola said that he stopped but he didn't come in. Instead, he went back down the stairs. Zeola remembers feeling a strange sense of relief but at the same time wondering what was going on. She wondered if he was coming back or what. Scared to move, she just lay there waiting and wondering until she became so exhausted she fell asleep. Needless-to-say, he never came back.

Zeola said that it took a long time to figure out why her father did what he did. Her final analogy of it seemed a bit unusual to me.

"In his mind he had already beaten me with mental torture. He did things like that to us sometimes. He enjoyed those mind games. I would have preferred the spanking."

"The spanking?" I screamed inside my head. *"You call making somebody strip and lay naked on a bed and get whipped with a leather strap a spanking? Sister girl, that is a beating!"* I wanted to yell aloud at her.

Generally, if she was being whipped Zeola said that Jeanne, Marvin and Frankie would be huddled together downstairs with their mom in fear for the one who was being whipped. Only this time nobody was home but her and her father.

I almost felt Zeola's despair while she was talking. It was as if she was reliving that whole incident, and I felt like I was there watching the two of them.

Zeola said that one time when she was little her father told her to come and sit on his lap and hug him, but instead of going to him, she looked to her mother. She remembers her mother encouraging her by saying, *"Go hug your father."* But she said she didn't want to do it. She said that she just couldn't do it.

I asked Zeola if she had ever been sexually abused by him, and she wasn't as forthcoming as I had hoped. She did, however, admit the possibility of sexual abuse, and tucked her head down like before, and said that she wasn't sure. She said that it might have been her father or her uncle she wasn't sure. Without looking at me she said that it may have happened when she was younger. She then quickly dismissed the subject and moved on to something else. But I wasn't finished with that issue. I knew that I would have to bring it up again in the future when she was in a different state of mind.

She went on to recall being scared to even have a conversation with her father. She said that if he were to ask her a question and her diction was not correct, or if she put a verb where a noun should be he would correct her harshly and make her feel terrible inside. She explained that it wasn't the fact that he corrected her, but it was the way he would do it. He also fussed at her for slouching.

"Sit up straight!" Zeola imitated her father and then laughed and said, "I guess I should have kept that one because I still slouch."

Even though Zeola said that she has blocked out most of her memories with her father, she still remembered the time he took her to the Cherry Blossom parade in Washington, DC. She recalled not wanting to go because she didn't feel comfortable being alone with him.

"I remember going to that parade so clearly. I even remember the checkered socks, peddle pushers and t-shirt that I wore. I remember wondering if Father would like my outfit. He could be so critical of us at times, so I approached him slowly. I wasn't sure if he would tell

me to go back upstairs and change clothes or just tell me that we weren't going because of the way I looked. Finally, I stiffened my shoulders, held my breath and entered the room where he was waiting, and I was so relieved when he only said, 'Are you ready to go?'"

That day Zeola also recalled her father instructing her to stand by a light pole so that he could take a picture of her. She said that she was about eight years old and remembers wanting to literally get up and run because she was sure that she would not do it right. Once again, she was waiting for his criticisms, but this time she figured she must have done something right because he didn't fuss at her.

Zeola says the last thing she remembers being alone with her father was when he was teaching her the abc's. She said he made her so nervous that she couldn't say them right. She knew that if he didn't spank her, he would fuss at her, and she said that she'd rather get a spanking than to hear that commanding tone in his voice. That superior voice that she said made her tremble with fear. Well, you know that once again my mind focused on that word, spanking. I don't think anybody in that family knew what a spanking was.

"I remember going to that parade so clearly. I even remember the checkered socks, peddle pushers and t-shirt that I wore. I remember wondering if Father would like my outfit. He could be so critical of us at times, so I approached him slowly. I wasn't sure if he would tell me to go back upstairs and change clothes or just tell me that we weren't going because of the way I looked. Finally, I stiffened my shoulders, held my breath and entered the room where he was waiting, and I was so relieved when he only said, 'Are you ready to go?'"

That day Zeola also recalled her father instructing her to stand by a light pole so that he could take a picture of her. She said that she was about eight years old and remembers wanting to literally get up and run because she was sure that she would not do it right. Once again, she was waiting for his criticisms, but this time she figured she must have done something right because he didn't fuss at her.

Zeola says the last thing she remembers being alone with her father was when he was teaching her the abc's. She said he made her so nervous that she couldn't say them right. She knew that if he didn't spank her, he would fuss at her, and she said that she'd rather get a spanking than to hear that commanding tone in his voice. That superior voice that she said made her tremble with fear. Well, you know that once again my mind focused on that word, spanking. I don't think anybody in that family knew what a spanking was.

"I remember one particular time when I got my abc's wrong, and Father beat me with a switch from a tree or a ruler, I can't remember which, and it broke the skin on both my hands. When he noticed that he had broken the skin and I was bleeding, he became that other person; that man who cared."

By now I had heard enough. I was ready to go to Gay Sr.'s grave and dig him up and curse him out. She really had my emotions stirred up. But I didn't say anything. I just allowed her to continue.

"Father said that he was really sorry. He apologized over and over again. I remember him going to get medical stuff to clean my cuts. He put medicine all over my hands and then made me lay in the bed while he went and got me some grapes and all the little things that he knew that I liked. He brought me soup and ice cream, and even gave me ginger ale. We never had another session like that again. Maybe he had been drinking when he hurt me, I don't know."

All that I could think of at that moment was, *"Alcohol is no excuse for that type of behavior."* I get so tired of hearing people use alcohol as an excuse for abuse. That is a crock of you-know-what.

After that long ordeal I became exhausted just listening to her. And when Zeola lit up what was left of her joint in the roach clip and took a small hit of it I was ready to snatch it out of her hand and hit it myself, but I knew better.

Zeola sunk back in the sofa cushions and stretched her legs out to get more comfortable, and then proceeded to talk again.

"I've got to give it up." She said with conviction. *"It's just been too long. I've got to tell it all."*

I waited to see if she had any more to say about the incident with the abc's but she appeared to be finished with that subject. So we moved on.

I wanted to know more about Gay Sr., so I asked Zeola if she knew why he was so strict. I asked her about his parents and where they came from and if they beat him the way he beat his children, and to my surprise, she had a lot to say about it.

"Father and his twelve brothers and two sisters were raised by their mother. He said that for punishment, she would tie them up, or hang them up by their arms and beat them with a wet board that had holes in it like they did in slavery days. He said that she had to do that because she had a lot of boys and she had to keep that respect in the family."

All that I could think of at that moment was how I wouldn't have let her do that to me. Respect or no respect, even though in the back of my mind I was sure that most offspring had little choice in the matters. Regardless, it is still hard for me to understand why our ancestors felt the need to beat their offspring the same way they had been beaten during slavery. If there is a method to that madness, I haven't figured it out yet because the very thought of stripping a child naked, and then beating the tar out of that defenseless kid would not get my respect in a million years. Instead, I think that it would anger the hell out of me, especially if I were that kid.

Since Zeola seemed to condone her father's actions, I asked her if she beat her children the way her father beat her. I asked that question because I had already met her two daughters, and they seemed like lovely young ladies. Zeola quickly responded. She said that she never beat her children that way. She said that somebody had to break that chain. She also said that her sisters and brothers did not abuse their kids either.

The moment Zeola used the word 'abuse' I knew that somewhere deep down in her heart she had accepted the fact that what Gay Sr. had been doing to them was undeniable 'abuse.' And that led me to believe her when she said that the chain of beatings in their family had truly been broken.

All I could think of at that point was, *"Thank God."*

CHAPTER
5

ALBERTA

WHY?
Why did Marvin's Father Shoot and Kill Him?

"When Father was in one of his good moods, I remember him telling us how beautiful he thought Maw was when he first saw her in that Pentecostal church. He said that he loved the way her hair hung down to her butt, and how he couldn't take his eyes off her beautiful big legs. My sister, Jeanne, probably knows more about how they got together. I just know that once they got married my mom said that she dedicated her life to becoming a full time minister's wife and mother."

Zeola said that she used to pat her mom on the back and tell her how much she admired her. *"I don't know how you do it, Maw."*

Even though Zeola seemed to defend and love her eccentric father, she realized just what a really good woman Alberta had to be to put up with him. She admired the fact that her mother never stopped trying to keep the peace in the family.

"She would try her best to make sure that we didn't put Father in a bad mood because he would fuss at us. She would tell us when we got home from school to make sure to go upstairs to his room and speak to him."

The smile on Zeola's face when she talked about her mother was always full of compassion and love.

'My mom seldom beat us. And when she did, she would use her little plastic belts with the cardboard backing. That didn't hurt, but we would act like we were really crying so that she wouldn't know that she wasn't hurting us. We tried not to do anything to get her upset because she was so sweet."

Alberta may have accepted a lot of abuse from Gay Sr., but she was not a passive kind of woman, according to Zeola. *"She would speak her mind. She would sometimes even talk back to him if it meant keeping us kids from getting a beating."*

Jeanne was the oldest of the kids, and Marvin was next. Sometimes Zeola said that she would look at Jean like she was her mom instead of her sister because Jeanne was left in charge of them whenever their parents weren't at home. But Marvin didn't see Jeanne that way. He would get into so many fights with her because he would challenge her on everything.

"Jeanne would win on physical stuff, but Marvin always won on mental challenges. Marvin loved the mind games."

Unlike their mother, Zeola felt that Jeanne didn't feel the same as the rest of the siblings when it came time for somebody to get a beating.

"She would tell on us in a minute."

Zeola said that she used to wonder if it was because Jeanne was the only one of them who looked like their father, that maybe she thought a little bit like him. But she said that she realizes now that that was the thoughts of a little girl who didn't know how to analyze things. However, when I asked her to analyze it now, she was still unable to do so. Even now it appears that she harbors some of the feelings of that little girl, but chooses not to admit it, and I understood, so I let it go.

"I love my sister, and I know that she loves me despite our childhood differences."

According to Zeola, the rest of them never told on each other. They felt that the less they set their father off the better.

"Whatever it took to keep him from going off on one of us we did it because depending on his mood or alcohol intake we could all end up getting a beating. Plus, the three of us just hated to see him hit any of us; including Jeanne. We feared him so much when we were little."

For a brief moment I felt a twinge of pity for Zeola. I saw that little girl nicknamed "Sweetsie" sitting in front of me. Her heart still seemed to ache from her past.

After a few minutes of silence I asked Zeola what she was thinking about, and she said that she hadn't finished talking about her sister, Jeanne. So I waited.

"Jeanne looked like Father, and Frankie sort of favored him too, but you could still see a little of Maw in him. Marvin and I always had Maw's features more so than Frankie and Jean. But as we've all gotten older things have changed. Frankie started looking more like Marvin and I am starting to look more like Jean."

Zeola smiled as she continued talking about Jeanne. She said that she remembered recently looking in the mirror and yelled out loud, *"Oh my God. I look like Jeanne. I don't want to look like my father."* She said that that's how much Jeanne looks like Gay Sr. She said that she was horrified. She made it clear that she was not making any negative remarks about Jeanne, but about her father.

"I always took pride in looking like my mom because she was such a good and loving person."

I told Zeola that I understood what she was saying, and we continued.

"Jean had all the good characteristics of Father as well." Zeola continued. *"She was smart and had the coldest body with the most beautiful legs I had ever seen. And most of all, she had the coldest walk you will ever see. My vow was to walk and write like my big sister. I used to go around the room prancing and practicing my walk so that I could walk like her. And she's still got the walk."*

When Zeola mentioned the walk it reminded me of the first time I met her. I said then that her sauntering reminded me of an old Mae West movie. Maybe she and Jeanne got their walk from Alberta. Although I never had the pleasure of meeting Alberta, I can almost envision this beautiful woman entering Gay Sr.'s church and taking his breath away by sauntering down the isle with her beautiful big legs and long curly hair.

I immediately convinced Zeola that she had said nothing negative about Jeanne so we continued.

"Father didn't work much. He was a traveling minister. However, he did take a job at the naval base in D.C. for a brief while where he drove the Naval officers around the compound. I guess he felt that being a traveling minister was enough, even though it didn't bring in very much money."

One day Zeola said she asked her mother why her father got to stay home and she had to go to work.

"Maw said that he had a back problem. She explained to me that he had a slipped disc in his back and wasn't able to work. That was bullshit, but I didn't know it at the time. All I knew was that my father stayed at home and fooled around with the neighborhood women while my mom worked, and that didn't seem right."

***

When Zeola was sixteen years old she said that she and her first boyfriend, George, used to sneak down in the basement of the house and have sex while her mother was upstairs.

"I guess I liked the thrill of sneaking even at that young age. But I was so naïve that I never thought about the consequences of what I was doing. I wasn't even enjoying the sex. I was just having fun sneaking. Father would be in the house too, but I seldom thought of him as being home because he stayed in his room most of the time."

Zeola remembered one time when she and George were in the basement playing around and her mom decided to come downstairs to talk with her. The minute Alberta called out, *"Sweetsie, are you down there?"* she said that her heart sank.

"I didn't know what to do, so I locked George in a tall skinny cabinet where we hung some of our clothes. I think we called it a wardrobe. The rich people call it an armoire. It's funny now, but it wasn't funny then because it seemed like it took forever for Maw to go back up those stairs. I felt so sorry for George because my mom never stopped talking."

Zeola said that every once in a while she would hear George bumping up against coat hangers.

"He couldn't sit down because there wasn't enough room. All I could think of was that the shit is really going to hit the fan if Maw finds George in that wardrobe-thing. I was so nervous. Generally, I enjoyed talking to Maw, but not that night. And I wouldn't dare tell her to go back upstairs. So I told her that I had to go to the bathroom, which was upstairs of course. And then I had to wait until she went into her bedroom and closed the door, and then hope and pray that Father wasn't sitting up in his usual place by his bedroom window. He sat there so that he could see who came in and who went out of our house. And he definitely would have seen George leaving."

Finally, in the middle of the night Zeola said that she tipped downstairs and let George out of the wardrobe.

"He had been closed up in that closet for almost six hours, and he was madder than hell at me."

Zeola and I chuckled the entire time she was telling me this part of her story. But I didn't know that this was just the beginning of another heart wrenching episode in her life.

"Shortly after that little incident my father left the ministry and I found out that I was pregnant. I was scared to tell anybody. So I asked one of my girlfriend's mothers to call my mom on the telephone and tell her that I was pregnant. When I got home my mom was waiting for me. She told me that I had to tell my father. I told her that I couldn't do that."

Alberta said, *"Sweetsie, you have to tell him."* Finally, Zeola said she told her father, and he said that she could not bring a baby in that house without a husband.

"So what was I supposed to do then? I did not want to marry George. I didn't even like him anymore. So my mother suggested an abortion and I agreed to it."

The thought of an abortion was kind of a relief for Zeola because the fear of the pain of giving birth was more than she said her little teenage mind could bear.

"I just could not imagine a whole baby coming out of that little hole down there between my legs. But little did I know that I was about to experience something much worse than the pain of having a baby or the fear of being put out of my father's house without a place to live."

In those days it was illegal to have abortions so everybody had to go to sleazy places with sleazy doctors. Sometimes they weren't even real doctors, especially the one that was referred to Zeola's mom.

"I can't remember why Maw didn't go with me to have the abortion. I just remember going downtown alone to a dark and smelly apartment building where this little ole Black man, dressed in a dirty ole medical coat, greeted me at the door with his hand extended for some money. I gave it to him immediately. I could feel him watching me as we walked toward his kitchen."

The supposedly doctor took an immediate liking to Zeola.

"I guess it was because I was still shapely and cute. I didn't look pregnant."

While they were walking Zeola said that she just couldn't help but wonder why it seemed so damp in that place. She said that she could almost swear that mold was literally growing in the corners of that nasty dark hallway.

"How could anybody live in such filth?" Zeola thought to herself. *"Father would never stand for a nasty house like this."*

Quietly this so-called doctor reached up in the kitchen cabinet and took out a bottle of Jack Daniels Whiskey and poured a whole shot of it in a glass and handed it to Zeola.

"Here, drink this." He said as he handed her the glass of whiskey.

Zeola didn't like the smell of it and told him that she didn't want it, but he insisted. He told her that it would relax her, and that it would take away some of the pain.

"Well, 'pain' was the key word. I certainly didn't want any of that, so I grabbed the glass and quickly swallowed every drop of it even though it tasted as badly as it smelled."

Shortly after that Zeola said that she did begin to relax a little bit.

"As a matter of fact, I think I was drunk because I couldn't seem to keep my balance when I tried to remove my panties. I remember thinking that I would keep my skirt on for protection. I don't know what sort of protection I was figuring on, but it sounded good at the time."

After persuading Zeola to drink the liquor, he told her that he had to have a sample of the moisture in her vagina, and that the only way that he could get it from her insides was to screw her.

"Well, I can't believe that I was so stupid, but I let him do it. What can I say? I was a sheltered kid. George was the only person that I had been with, and I was scared to death of this old man. I thought that I was supposed to do whatever he told me to do. A sixteen year old girl back then was different from what a sixteen year old girl is like today. Kids know more about everything these days. Television has taught them a lot. Plus, parent talk to their kids more today than they did then."

At first, Zeola said that she thought that the man was making a mistake in touching her breast as he reached under her armpits to help her up on to that hard wooden table, but by the time she left that day she said that she knew that he intended to do just what he did.

"I still remember what that beady-eyed little creep's cold hands felt like when he touched me. He reminded me of Quasi Moto when Quasi Moto fell in love with that girl in that movie."

The doctor said, *"Now, I am going to have to tie your wrists down so that you don't panic and make me cut you by mistake, okay?"* Zeola said that she did not want him to tie her down and she told him so, but he politely insisted, and like a dummy, she gave in to his request.

"All the time he was cutting the gauze and gently tying my wrists to the legs of the table with that gauze, he kept assuring me that everything would be okay."

Somehow the fact that he was small in stature and had a real soft voice, Zeola said that it made him less intimidating. She said that he just didn't look like somebody who would deliberately harm her, so she cooperated with him.

"I recall keeping my head turned to the side and staring at the dingy colored sheet that covered the table that I was lying on. I just didn't want to see what he was doing. And I certainly didn't want to focus on that big cockroach that had strolled out of the same kitchen cabinet where he got the liquor."

Zeola remembered her legs trembling as they were stretched wide open and propped up on some sort of boxes with some homemade stirrups for her feet.

"There wasn't even a sheet thrown over, or anything. I was laying there bare-assed with my skirt pulled up to my waist, my wrists tied to the table and this grubby little man standing on a wooden box between my legs looking at me like he was about to feast

on a Thanksgiving turkey. All I could do was cry and close my eyes and hope that this terrible nightmare would soon end."

When Zeola first felt his cold hands rub some sort of grease over her vagina, she said that she wandered what it was that he was putting on her, but she was too afraid to ask.

"I just squeezed my eyes tighter, and bit my lip harder and waited terrifyingly for whatever was coming next."

"Hold still now," He said softly as he slowly and methodically penetrated her vagina with his penis. "This will only take a minute."

Zeola said that she just could not believe what she had gotten herself into. She said that she started crying so hard that her whole body started trembling.

"Now that I look back on it, I probably excited him even more so with all the jerking and trembling that I was doing."

I have mentioned before how Zeola can sometimes give the impression of a soft-spoken and sweet little girl, and that is who I felt I was listening to at this time. I found myself almost wanting to find that nasty little bastard and beat his head against one of those dark and dingy walls that surrounded that filthy kitchen.

When I asked Zeola why her mother didn't go with her, she couldn't remember. I figured Gay Sr. probably kept Alberta from going.

"Just a little bit more… He groaned as he grind on top of me and ran those chilly little fingers over my stomach and my breast. Just a little bit more… He kept whispering. Finally, after he was finished doing his shit inside of me there was complete silence, so I slowly opened my eyes to see what was going on. I had cried so many tears that everything looked blurred, but I could see enough to know that he didn't seem to be in the room. So I relaxed a little."

A few seconds later Zeola said that she felt a bit of warm air between her legs.

"When I lifted my head up to see what was going on down there all that I could see was the top of this man's head buried between my thighs. It was his breath that I was feeling on my vagina!"

Zeola explained that the man was bending down, smelling her with his eyes closed.

"What are you doing?" She yelled. And before he could say anything else she said that she took her foot out of that stupid stirrup thing and kicked him up side his head and pushed him off that box and on to the floor.

"I was so mad. I had had enough of that shit. It was at that moment I knew that this was not the way an abortion was supposed to work, and I wasn't going to hang around there another minute. I quickly worked my hands out of the ties, jumped off that big ole table and grabbed my purse and stormed out of that hell-hole without my panties."

Zeola said that the bus ride home was the longest ride of her life. She said that she did not want to even look at anybody.

"It felt like everybody on that bus knew that I didn't have any panties on, and I had cried so much that my eyes were almost swollen shut. After I got home I didn't know what to say to my mom, so I just went to my room and got under the covers and stayed there for the rest of the day and well into the night until everybody went to bed. Finally, I got up and went into the bathroom and practically washed the skin off my body. I just couldn't get rid of the mildew smell of that dingy sheet that covered that table."

The next day Zeola said that she broke down and told her mom that she just chickened out.

"There was no way that I could tell her what I had let that man do to me. It was too embarrassing. And needless to say, I never did

get an abortion, and until this very day, I can't stand the thought of having sex with older men."

The following week Zeola said that Marvin called from Detroit and she told him that she was pregnant and he went off on her really bad. She said that he hurt her feelings worse than her father did.

"He actually sounded like Father."

Marvin called her a whore and asked her where her morals were, and what was she thinking. She remembers not being able to stop crying.

"I wondered what he would have said if he had known what happened in that doctor's house."

While Zeola was talking I could almost feel her pain. She loved Marvin so much and it was as if he was here with us, and calling her names all over again.

"I became so depressed because George didn't want to get married. We were just kids."

Finally, she said that George called her. She said that she had already told him what her father had said, but this time she told him what Marvin had called her, so he decided to marry her. She was eight months pregnant.

"He didn't even come home the night of the wedding. He stayed out with his girlfriend, and I cried all that night. And from that day on there was never a peaceful moment between us."

George was really mean, Zeola said. I could see the pain in her face as she continued to talk about him. She said that he hit her in the eye one time, so her mother put him out of their house. After she had the baby, she ended up moving in with his parents. She said that his mother and his sister hated her guts. And even though they did not get along, she said that he still wanted sex every night.

"George raped me every night. I used to cry the whole time he raped me, so he would put the pillow over my head and tell me to move. It got to the point where his mother would holler down the hall for us to stop making so much noise. I know that legally when two people are married you cannot cry rape, but as far as I was concerned, if this was being done to me without my permission, it was rape. I felt so violated. One time I got up and called my mom and I was crying so hard that she told me to get the baby and come home. So that's what I did. I picked up Nikki and wrapped her in a blanket and I went home."

That night, Zeola said that her father came downstairs in the basement while she was washing clothes, and he asked her if she had asked his permission to come home and she told him that she had not.

"I told him that Maw said I could come home. So he went upstairs and I could hear him and my mom arguing. And then he came back downstairs and asked me if I loved him. I told him that I didn't know. That was my first time ever talking back to him and it felt really good. He got so mad he told me to get my baby and all my stuff and get out of his house. I remember crying again because I didn't know where to go. I could hear my mom pleading with Father to let me stay. He was yelling at her and asking her what kind of kids did she have that they didn't love him. Finally, after I had packed everything and bundled my baby up in my arms, he came in my room and told me not to take that baby out in that kind of weather. That was his way of saying that I could stay. Once again, my mom had come through."

By now Alberta was beginning to sound like a saint to me. My heart continuously went out to her for dealing with so much grief and heartache with this horrible man.

As protective as Marvin was of Zeola, she said that he was twenty times more protective of her mother. She said that the

Gay children all felt that it was time for Alberta to be protected and enjoy whatever was left of her life.

"She shouldn't have been hassled by our Father the way she had been. She deserved better." Zeola said sharply. *"I used to tell her all the time that she deserved a metal for putting up with Father all those years."*

Zeola imitated her mother's reply by saying, *"Sweetsie, sometimes it's better to just keep the peace. It doesn't matter if you bend. God sees what you're doing."*

Zeola insisted that her mother only stayed with her father for the sake of the children even though Alberta said that it was because she didn't believe in divorce.

"She stuck with him all the way up until Marvin's death. I was always so proud of how strong and beautiful she remained."

Most Black women in Washington DC didn't have much education back in the 50's and 60's so they either cleaned houses or worked for the government. The ones that had a little schooling got the government jobs, but Zeola said that Alberta was only qualified to clean houses for the rich people over in Virginia.

"It embarrassed me a little bit knowing that my mother cleaned white people's houses, but because most of the mothers that we knew did it, it wasn't too bad. By the time I got to Jr. High School people stopped calling it 'day work' and called it 'domestic cleaning.' I liked that better. It presented a better image. I would say, 'My mother is a domestic worker.' That sounded real good to me."

Every day Marvin and Frankie would wait to carry Alberta's bags from the bus stop.

"She would always bring us food that was left over from whatever she cooked for the white folks. At Christmas and holidays we got to have turkey and a lot of other good stuff. We just couldn't

have pork or anything in a shell like shrimp and lobster because of our religion. All of our meats had to be Kosher."

Sometimes Alberta would take Zeola to work with her. Zeola said that Marvin and Frankie didn't go very often. She said that she was taken because she was the baby. I reminded her that the others probably didn't go because they were in school. She said that she hadn't thought of that. We both concluded that the others probably went when they were preschool as well.

"I remember how maw would go to sleep on the bus when I went to work with her. I would always be so worried that we would pass our stop because I never knew where we were going. And sometimes Maw would snore. That's when I would get so embarrassed. I remember hoping that somebody would ring a bell or make some noise that would wake her up, but she would never wake up until it was time to get off that bus. Somehow she always knew when to wake up."

Zeola said that she loved being at work with her mother because she would get to play with the rich kid's toys. She said that she thinks her mother enjoyed having her there and seeing her play with real toys because they only had homemade toys at the Gay house.

"I especially liked it when the owners weren't there. I used to pretend that we lived there, and all the beautiful things belong to us."

Being on the job with her mother also enabled Zeola to see just how hard her mother worked.

"She never made me do too much to help her. I guess I was too small to do much of anything. She might ask me to go and get something once in a while or hang something out on the clothes line, but I didn't do much more than that. And because I was raised not to touch things she never had to worry about me doing anything

wrong. I didn't touch anything I wasn't supposed to touch. Maw would always say that I was a sweet child. She used to say that I was the best child she ever had. She told me that was why they named me Sweetsie. I liked my nickname. Some family members still call me Sweetsie."

Zeola said that when she was little she never understood why her mother had to get up, cook breakfast, dress the kids, get fussed at by their father and then get on a bus in the cold D.C. weather and go to somebody else's house to clean up their mess. And then come home tired and drained, and have to prepare dinner and then put the kids to bed.

"When Father drank we never knew what kind of mood he would be in. His mood determined whether he would make Maw's evening pleasant or just plain miserable."

***

Zeola explained that before Alberta married Gay Sr., she gave birth to a son named Michael, and Gay Sr. never let her forget that she had had a child out of wedlock.

"When my parents got married Father wouldn't allow Michael to stay in our house. He had to go and live with Aunt Zeola. This caused a lot of bitterness between my father and Michael and my aunt. They couldn't understand how my father could be so mean."

Whenever Gay Sr. was in one of his nasty moods, he would throw up the birth of Michael to Alberta. Zeola said that he would call her a slut and tell her how she should be ashamed of herself for having an illegitimate son. She said that Gay Sr. would say anything that he thought might bring Alberta down, and she would take it. Most of the time Zeola said that her mom wouldn't fuss back or anything.

"I always knew about Mike, and that he was my brother, but I didn't understand how that came about until I was about fourteen or fifteen when I would go and stay with Aunt Zeola in Detroit and she

would talk about him. By this time Mike was in jail. According to Aunt Zeola he was a known hit man in Detroit."

Zeola said that she always thought that Mike was so gorgeous. She said that she used to dream about him, but would never tell anybody because he was her half brother. She said that it felt sort of strange. She said that she never had dreams about Marvin or Frankie because they were her brothers, but Mike didn't feel like a real brother. Even though he was tall like Marvin and he looked liked Alberta, Zeola said that he didn't favor any of the other kids. She said that he was very light like Alberta and he had a lot of freckles.

"I have always been fascinated with the mafia shit, and Mike reminded me of them because he was so cold-blooded and tough. He didn't take any shit. I just admired how tough he was, and he was so handsome. Of course he never knew that. I just kept it to myself. "

Zeola said that Michael saved her life one time, and she didn't even know it until much later.

After Zeola became an adult and had kids of her own she said that she felt that she could do whatever she wanted to do even though she was living at home.

"I had this boyfriend who was a burglar. He broke into people's houses and I used to sit in the car and be the lookout girl. If I saw somebody coming I would blow the horn. I really liked this guy. I am so blessed that I didn't land in prison. I don't know to this day why I did that. I think it was probably for the excitement. I am just so grateful to God that I never got arrested because I really liked this guy a lot and did some dumb stuff for him."

Zeola said that one time when she was in a nightclub an older man hit on her. She said that he was a numbers backer. I had never heard of a backer, so I asked her what that meant and she explained that back in the day people played the numbers illegally in D.C., and numbers backers were known to be very wealthy. I still did not understand, until she explained that backers put up the front money for the gamblers who played the numbers.

"This guy invited me over to his house so I went with him. He had a really nice place. I remember him giving me about three or four hot dresses. I will never forget this one dress. It was bad! It had silver zippers that came down the front of it. Anyway, he asked me to come down in the basement because he wanted to show me something. He showed me a suitcase full of money. I had never seen so much money in my life."

Zeola said that word got back to her boyfriend, Puggy, that she was over this man's house and Puggy became furious. So she said that she told him that she had heard that he had a lot of money in his house and she was there to check him out and set him up.

"Puggy and his cousin decided that they were going to go in the man's house and get the money. But apparently this man paid for police protection and Puggy didn't know that the cops would ride past this man's house every ten or fifteen minutes. So, instead of Puggy going after the money like he should have been doing, he decided to go after the man because the man tried to hit on me."

Zeola said that Puggy ended up shooting the man in the leg and crippling him, and was sent to jail for doing it. After that she said that they broke up.

On that note, I was almost ready to stop the audio tape recorder. This story was getting to be too much for me. I didn't know whether to write this down or report her to the police. I didn't think that she should be telling this sort of thing, especially to be written in a book where everybody would read about it, but she said that she wanted to 'give it up.' So I recorded it all, and continued to take my notes.

As a result of all of this Zeola said that a contract was put out on her. But luckily her brother Mike was hired to do it, and he told them that she was his sister and that nothing had better happen to her.

At this point, once again, I was ready to ask Zeola for a hit of her joint to calm me down because this was too much drama for me. But of course I didn't do it. I knew better.

"I always thought Mike was so handsome, and he always acknowledged me as his baby sister. I just thought he was so cool. I still get chills when I think about how I almost got killed in the 60's. I am still grateful to my half brother for looking out for me. I don't think I ever told him just how grateful I was. And in case I didn't, I'm saying it now. Thank you, Michael, for being my brother and having my back."

Michael was always in trouble growing up, and Zeola said that she believes that it was because he didn't have their mother there to be with him.

"Father wouldn't even allow her to visit him in jail. But sometimes Mike came to see us when he would get out of jail. I still get sad sometimes when I think about how he was treated. He didn't deserve any of that."

Zeola said that Mike finally got himself together and started working at one of the car plants in Detroit and has since retired. She said that he is now married with several beautiful children, probably grandchildren too.

Cooking and cleaning their house was what Alberta liked to do best, according to Zeola.

"It probably came from when she had to do it all the time in D.C. If you would go to my mother's house any time of the day or night, there would always be food in the kitchen. Everybody looked forward to Maw's cooking. They even called her Maw or Mother. Nobody called her Mrs. Gay."

Zeola said that her mother could be very funny sometimes.

"I remember her telling us a joke. She didn't tell them too well, but this one was funny, especially coming from her. She told us about a preacher passing the bread and wine around in Holy Communion, and this drunk was sitting in the back of the church. She said that the minister passed the bread first and said, 'As you eat this bread it is the symbol of the Lord's body. And eat that in remembrance of him.' So she said that everybody ate the bread. And then they passed the wine around and before you drink it you wait for the minister to say something again. So the minister said, 'And this wine that you are about to drink is Jesus' blood. So drink that in remembrance of him.' So, Maw said that the drunk drank the wine and then hollered out 'Kill 'em again!'"

Well, once again I wasn't sure if this was something that I should include in this book in fear of offending some religions, but Zeola felt that it was okay at the time of our session. She felt that it was quite funny, and thought that it will be conceived as funny by the readers because she couldn't imagine anyone thinking that her mother would ever intentionally offend anybody.

I somewhat agreed with her point of view because I may have never met this lady, but her love for her family definitely has touched my heart a few times during these sessions.

"After we came to California Maw tried again to deal with Father. She would talk to him about not wanting to go anywhere, or not wanting to hang out with us. But after she had talked and talked she finally realized that Father wasn't going to change, so she didn't seem to give a damn anymore."

***

Zeola said that she felt that her mom knew about her father fooling around with the little girl up the street.

"She used to come down to the house and go up in Father's room and close the door. I heard that I even have a little brother as a result of that mess. I don't know what his name is, but her name is Sheila. Even in D.C. he had a little girl. My mom was so cool she even watched that baby a few times, I think. She was unbelievable. Maw probably let her in our house. But the girl didn't come around when I was home. I wouldn't have said anything to my father, but you had better believe that I would have made her feel very uncomfortable."

After so many years of marriage, Zeola said that her mother just got tired of trying.

***

Marvin loved having Maw on the road with him. Zeola said that he would also make sure that she brought one of her friends so that she wouldn't be lonely.

"Besides this country Maw traveled with us to Europe, Jamaica, Japan and Hawaii, and Marvin always found a place for her to stay where there was a stove so that she could cook her wonderful fried chicken and greens for him. And she loved doing it. Father declined all of these trips. It finally got to a point where nobody cared."

Zeola recalled an incident in San Francisco where the people were boycotting outside the venue of one of Marvin's shows. She said that she thinks that they were boycotting the promoters, but she wasn't sure. She said that this was around the time of the album Let's Get It On. She said that a lot of tickets were not sold and Marvin's feelings were hurt because the venue was not filled with people.

"Marvin had a pretty big ego, and wasn't going to perform. My mother was backstage at the time. She came to a lot of Marvin's concerts. She told Marvin that he should go out there and perform. She said that she didn't care if there were ten people out there. She said that was ten more people who loved him, and he looked at Maw

with the admiration of a little boy, and he hugged her and kissed her and then put on one hellava show.

Zeola said that her mother started complaining about pain in her legs and her joints. So Marvin wanted her checked out before going out on the next tour. He put her in Brotman Hospital where they ran tests and drew bone marrow. That's when Marvin found out that Alberta had cancer.

"From that point on Marvin was full of anxiety. That sort of started his demise. It was almost the beginning of the end for Marvin."

Marvin instructed the doctors not to tell Alberta that she had cancer, according to Zeola. The doctor supposedly said that this was the most painful type of malignant cells. Zeola said that the doctor described the pain that Alberta would be experiencing as if something was literally eating right into the bone of her leg. And if somebody were to pull her mother too hard or hold her too tight her bones could possibly break.

"Marvin just didn't want her to know that the doctors had said that her bones would become brittle like eggshells, so he told me, not to tell anybody else. Nobody knew that she had cancer but the doctors and Marvin and me."

Right after Alberta's diagnoses Zeola said that things started to go down hill for Marvin. After becoming very depressed, she said that he couldn't stop talking to her about their mother's death.

"All that he would talk about on that last tour was Maw's cancer. And every now and then when she would start feeling real sick, Marvin would worry even more. All he ever wanted to do was to make her happy because Father made her life so miserable. He said that he didn't think he could handle Maw's death. He said that Maw could probably handle his death better than he could handle hers."

Zeola said that her mother's cancer had gone quite a long time before coming back, but "Right after Marvin was killed the cancer resurfaced." Up until then Zeola said that nobody knew about it accept her and Marvin. She said that her mother started experiencing so much pain that Jeanne took her to the doctor and that's when the doctor told Jeanne about it and said that Alberta only had 6 months to live.

"My mom always said that if there was anybody in her life who would take care of her when she got too sick or too old she thought it would be Jeanne. Jeanne liked to stay at home. She didn't like going on tour; even when Maw went. She was somewhat of a prude, but she was smart."

Needless-to-say, they were all devastated with the diagnosis. Zeola said that all they could do was cry. She said that they had already lost Marvin, and now they were about to lose the other most precious person in their lives.

Jeanne and Frankie took it really hard. But Zeola said that she just kept having faith that her mother would not die in 6 months, even though she did want her out of her misery.

"And she didn't die in 6 months. She lasted so long that the doctors said that they weren't even going to predict her death again because she had made a liar out of them too many times."

I did not get a chance to ask Zeola for more details about her mother's illness or how long she persevered because we never got around to it before Zeola left the project. But she had said that even though her mother wasn't getting any better, Alberta was still hanging in there because of so much love and prayer surrounding her.

"I never understood why anybody that sweet and loving and caring should go through so much pain before dying." Zeola said as she let out a tearful sigh.

CHAPTER
6

SPIRITUAL ENCOUNTER

The first time I became aware of a spiritual presence connected with this book was shortly after I started working with Zeola.

In the beginning I noticed that when I stacked research papers regarding Marvin on my desk or placed old Hollywood magazines that contained articles about him on the table they would either fall to the floor for no reason or literally move to the other side of my desk when I wasn't looking. I remember wondering why this was happening. I remember looking under the table to see if the legs were uneven, and they were not. I checked the books and magazines to see if they were stacked improperly, but nothing seemed out of the ordinary. So I continued to work, and I never connected it with anything other than a crazy fluke. It was several weeks before I began to realize that something amazing was happening to me.

After only a short period of time working with Zeola the lack of advanced funding was causing my pocket book to take a serious beating. I started out with a little savings in the bank, but it was dwindling fast.

Frustrated by the inability to decide what to do about Zeola, I sat at my dinner table most of the evening picking at my lasagna and weighing the pro's and con's of continuing with a project that I suspected could possibly take at least 6 months to a year to complete. I looked over at my dishwasher that needed repairs and wondered how I was going to pay for it, but at the same time I knew that I could live without a dishwasher. I wasn't that spoiled. Besides, I only use it when I have guests over for dinner. But then I thought about my car needing servicing, and that definitely was a necessity, but I couldn't afford to get that done either. I sat there so long that my food got cold. Finally, I dumped my dinner in the disposal and flipped the switch to turn it on, and I immediately became grateful that at least the disposal worked. I then cleaned up my dishes and went to bed.

When I walked into my bedroom and switched on my bedside lamp, the light bulb started to flicker. Once again a pang of anxiety raced through my upper body. I thought, *"Here is something else that needs fixing."* I couldn't even bare the thought of purchasing something as simple as a tiny light bulb during that time, not to mention the possibility of a broken lamp. Although my tiny touch-sensitive bedside light had little monetary value, I wasn't quite ready to part with it.

In order to turn the lamp on and off you must touch the brass base. The first touch creates a low mood glow, and the second touch creates a brighter 60 watt light. If you touch it a third time the lamp is suppose to turn off. While the low light was flickering, I touched it a second time in hopes that it would stop flickering and get brighter, and it did. But on the third touch it was suppose to turn off, and it did not. It just remained bright.

Since childhood I have preferred sleeping with a low light on in my bedroom, so I tried touching the brass base several times in an effort to dim the light, but to no avail. Frustrated, I finally reached over the side of my bed and snatched the plug right out of the wall socket, and turned over and closed my eyes in an attempt to go to sleep. But that didn't work either because the whole issue of whether I should or should not proceed with this lengthy project kept racing through my head.

After finally making my decision not to write the book, I felt relieved and decided not to think about it anymore. I just could not afford the luxury. And even though I was home alone, I announced aloud that I was not going to write the book. *"I just can't afford to do that right now,"* I blurted out aloud, and then pulled my favorite comforter up over my head and once again closed my eyes. I had finally convinced myself that I could not survive financially, and I was okay with that decision. But my eyes did not stay closed very long because moments later I sensed something happening outside my covers. Quickly I pulled the comforter off my face, and to my dismay, that darned unplugged lamp light was flashing on and off again, almost as if it was sending me some sort of code. Startled beyond one's imagination, I quickly sat up in the bed with my eyes wide open, staring at the light. I probably looked like something straight out of a cartoon movie because my eyes felt like they were the size of tea cup saucers. And just as quickly as the light started flashing, it stopped.

Finally, after I got myself together I looked over the side of my bed to see if the lamp was really unplugged, and it was. At that moment I decided that the only logical answer was that I must have been dreaming. So I calmed myself down, slid back under the covers determined not to come out until morning.

The next day when I woke up I was pleased to find the lamp still out of commission. I wasn't as frazzled as I had been the night before so I decided to plug it in and touch the brass base to see what would happen. Well, it lit up on low wattage nicely, so I touched it again and it got brighter like it was suppose to, and finally, on the third stroke it went out just as it should have.

Satisfied that everything was back to normal and that I must have been dreaming, I decided to go on with my plans for the day.

I immediately proceeded down the hall to my linen closet to retrieve a towel and wash cloth. But when I returned, to my dismay, I found that darned lamp proudly lit again at low wattage as if teasingly waiting for me to respond. Determined not to allow this creepy little inanimate object get the best of me, I immediately decided to dismiss its very presence and go quickly into the bathroom, close the door and take my shower. When I got out of the shower, I hesitated before exiting my bathroom because I dreaded the thought of that lamp waiting for me. But to my surprise when I came out and looked at it, the light had gone out. So I got dressed and left the house without addressing the possibility of it ever happening again. But, unusual occurrences continued to transpire throughout the ordeal of writing this book.

A spiritual presence became more and more obvious as time went on. It never failed that one of Marvin's songs would come on the radio as soon as I began to write, or the lights would flicker or some other bazaar incident would occur. At first I thought that it was a mere coincidence that the radio would play his songs while I was working. I compared it with a situation such as buying a car. Somehow you never seem to notice a particular model of car until you purchase one, and then suddenly you see them everywhere. I felt that I was only noticing the frequency of Marvin's songs on the radio because I had started working on this book. However, I could not explain the misplaced papers or the flickering lights.

I will never forget the time when I was sitting at my desk in my office listening to the recordings that Zeola and I had made at the previous session, when something brushed lightly across the outer part of my left leg about six inches below the bend in my knee. It felt as if a fly or a gnat or a very small insect was crawling across the hair on my leg. I swiped at it and then continued listening to the tapes assuming that I had made whatever it was go away, but that didn't work.

Moments later I felt it again, so I swatted at it again. This time I made sure to lightly smack the palm of my hand against my leg. That way, I figured if something was crawling on me it would not live to do it again. But that didn't work either. This time it had moved higher up the side of my leg closer to my knee.

The hairs on my legs are so sparse that I have never needed to shave them, of which I am most grateful, and there is even less hair closer to my knee. So, when I felt this movement on an area that was even more sensitive to the touch I went crazy with aggravation. This time I did more than swat at it. I smacked my leg so hard that it stung and left the red print of my hand. I could not believe that I had hit myself that hard, but at least I knew that I had killed that pesky thing. But, to my disappointment, I had not accomplished a darned thing. Within about fifteen minutes, after the sting had faded, and I had finally relaxed and started working, I felt it again.

"This is ridiculous!" I yelled aloud as I quickly bent over in hopes of locating the little varmint that had invaded my personal territory. Plus, I was determined not to let it travel any higher. After closely inspecting the almost invisible follicles of hair on my leg, I proceeded to check out the carpet on the floor. The most I had seen in my home was an occasional spider crawling on the wall or a silverfish in the bathroom sink, and the very thought of any one of those creatures crawling up my leg was too much for me to bear. So I thought maybe some sort of microscopic bug was doing this, but that made me even crazier because I hate bugs. I instantly tried to recall the last time that I had vacuumed the room, thinking that maybe some sort of insects had invaded the carpet, but I had just cleaned everything the previous

weekend. So I diligently started looking for the blasted invader, but to no avail, I couldn't find a thing. My last resort was to quickly get in the shower in an attempt to wash away whatever was disrupting my session. Needless-to-say, I never went back to writing that day, and the sensation never returned.

At our next meeting I told Zeola about the frustrations of that day, and her only comment was that Marvin always did like big legs, and was probably feeling up on mine. Although we both laughed at the possibility, I still made sure after that to wear pants when I worked on this project.

At one point not long after the leg incident I became very uneasy and considered discontinuing the writing sessions because I felt that all of these strange incidents might be signs telling me to stop. I mentioned it to Zeola who understood my concerns, but convinced me that it was alright to proceed. She said that she too had been visited by a spiritual entity, which she believed to be the spirit of Marvin. She knew that I was of a spiritual nature, so she said that working on this project probably invited him into my spiritual realm. She also made a joke about how Marvin loved women, and was probably just messing with me. I'm not quite sure if I found the joke to be funny, but since spiritual encounters are not totally foreign to me, I was not spooked by the possibility. I just continued to wear my pants.

After a few more unexplainable incidents, I finally got to a point where I made sure to turn the radio off, leave no papers or books stacked high, and write only during the day so that my lights wouldn't flicker.

There was, however, a time that I was privy to share a flickering light incident with someone. It was when I visited a black owned recording studio in Hollywood in an effort to pitch Zeola's idea for a movie. I felt very comfortable going there because I had been referred by a good friend who came along with me. When my friend introduced me to the young and well dressed African American gentleman and I shook his hand I should have left that office right then because I did not get a good vibe from his touch. But I just assumed that it was because of the many years of working with studio executives who are generally uptight and aggressive.

The young brother seemed very receptive to my idea, however, after a while a little corner of my mind told me that I should be careful because this is 'Hollywood,' and people steal ideas in movie town. Also, my antenna should have gone up when he decided that he did not want the record company that he worked for to hear my idea, but that he wanted to do it on his own. He said that the owner's wife was the person who operated the film portion of the record company, and he did not want to give it to her because the power would be taken away from him.

My feeling at that moment was one of discomfort because here he was sitting in the board room of his employer and requesting that I make a deal with him under the table for my story, and I had only just been introduced to him.

He said that he was trying to become a film producer, and that this would give him that opportunity. He promised to raise the necessary funds, and get the correct people involved. But the fact that he did not speak well of the company he was representing, and he had only known me less than one hour made me suspicious, so I asked him to sign a confidentially agreement.

During our discussion, I noticed that one of the recessed ceiling lights in the conference room started slowly blinking off and on. At first I sort of ignored it, but after a while the flashing became more and more obvious.

At one point during my pitch, the young man left the room to retrieve a pen and some paper to sign the agreement, and that's when the light started flickering off and on, faster and faster. All that I could equate it to was the flickering of the bedside lamp in my bedroom the night I decided not to write the book.

Finally, I told my friend and associate to look at the light in the ceiling. Jokingly, I told her that it must be Marvin telling me something, but I didn't know whether he was telling me to stay or leave that office, and we both laughed. I then brought her up to date on the previous flickering lights and paranormal incidents that had occurred. She only stared at me as if I had truly lost my mind. The instant the guy came back into the room with his pen and paper, the light immediately stopped blinking, and my associate gave me another strange look as if to say that maybe there was something to what I was talking about, and she appeared to be a bit spooked.

Unfortunately, I wasn't able to decipher that the flickering light was a sign to shut my mouth and get the hell out of that office. Instead, I stayed and talked too much about my story. And to make it worse, I ended up bringing my attorney to a later meeting with this man. Needless-to-say, my attorney was not impressed, and we did not proceed.

The next time I heard from this 'brother' he explained to me that he had decided that he did not want to do the story because he had thought about it, and since he had been wanting to get next to Nona, Marvin's daughter, for such a very long time, this would hurt his chances.

Other than Zeola and my associate, he was the only person who knew that I possessed the hand-written letter that Marvin had sent to Jan. So when Zeola called me to tell me that she had been paid not to continue with the book, she also told me that someone had told Jan about the hand written letter. Of course, my first reaction was that it had to have been this ambitious jerk. From then on I have paid close attention to flickering lights, and anything else that seemed to occur out of the ordinary. I have always known that signs are there for a reason, and I generally pay attention, but after this book I have become even more mindful of the paranormal.

CHAPTER
7

Photo by Bill Jones

MARVIN

"Marvin first started smoking cigarettes while he attended Cardozo High School in Washington DC. The last city bus stop was about three houses from ours on 60thstreet, so the bus drivers would sometimes sit there until it was time for them to go in. Marvin would bum cigarettes from them almost every day. And when he thought that he had asked for too many, he would send for me. He would say, "Sweetsie, go out there and get me a cigarette." And I would go out there with my cute little self and come back with the goods every time because Marvin had taught me just how to ask for whatever I wanted."

Zeola said that Marvin was good at understanding body language and sensuality. She said that she never stopped being amazed at him. Even at a young age she said that he had a winning way with people. Right after that she reminded me of her earlier statement about his charm not always working with his sister Jeanne. *"She didn't allow Marvin to get away with anything."* This was probably because she was the oldest and knew him best.

Everybody wondered how Marvin got A's because he never studied like the rest of the kids. He hardly ever brought books home from school, and whenever he did, Zeola said that he would lose them.

"Maw would always end up having to pay for new books over and over again. I remember her getting really frustrated with Marvin one time. She asked him how he remained an 'A' student without studying, and Marvin replied, "I'm a genius! What can I say?"

Zeola and I both laughed at that statement because her vivid descriptions of Marvin made it easy to envision this wonderful little kid telling his mother this with such conviction.

80

"Maw didn't know what to say after that. She just walked away and hid her face so that he wouldn't see her laughing." Zeola said as she smiled like Marvin. It was interesting how much she resembled him at times.

"I remember Marvin telling my mom when we were little kids that he had had this dream where he performed in front of millions of people and changed their lives with his music. My mom told him that if that's what he dreamed then that's what will probably happen. She told him that he should always believe in his dreams. Marvin told her that he couldn't wait to make a lot of money so that she wouldn't have to work anymore."

Zeola said that her mother, Alberta was the love of Marvin's life and he couldn't stand the way their father treated her.

"One day when Marvin was about seventeen years old, my father was upstairs arguing with Maw and Marvin jumped up and told him to stop talking to her like that. Well, Father could not believe that Marvin had done that so it became a really big mess."

Frankie and Zeola were downstairs and heard their mother say, *"No doc, don't hit him! Don't hit him!"*

"My father had grabbed a hammer from what I can remember, and he was going to hit Marvin with it. I remember trembling all over at the sound of Father's voice. I knew that he would have killed Marvin that very night if Marvin hadn't left the house. My mom knew it too. That's why she told Marvin to leave the house."

Zeola said that her father felt that Marvin not only disrespected him as a man and a father and the head of the household, but Marvin had interfered with his marriage.

"To Father that was the ultimate no-no. He ran his house the way he thought a house should be run."

Jeanne had already moved out of the house and joined the Air Force. Zeola said that she believed that Jeanne's leaving was for similar reasons. She didn't remember a confrontation between Jeanne and her father, but she said that her mother had told her that a similar disagreement with Gay Sr. had ensued.

"When Marvin started grabbing his personal things and preparing to leave and Father was fussing and yelling and telling him to get out, it felt like my world was just about to end. I loved my brother very much and I couldn't imagine existing without him. He was my confidant, my hero in shining armor and my sensitive and strong big brother who dared anybody to harm me. I am sure that Frankie and Maw felt something similar because we were all crying uncontrollably."

Marvin joined the Air Force right after that, which to Zeola was the beginning of a love-hate relationship between him and their father.

"I think Father finally realized just how much love we all had for each other over him. But he just couldn't change the way he had been all of his life."

Many writers tell of Marvin's rebellious attitude while he was in the Air Force.

"That was probably one of the few things that they wrote that was close to the truth about Marvin because he did resent authority."

Zeola said that both Jean and Marvin joined another branch of the Air Force called the paratroopers, but said that Marvin had a problem taking orders there too. I had not heard this before, and I'm not sure if Zeola got it right, but she insisted that I write it.

"The sergeants couldn't get him to do anything. It was totally amazing that he even got an honorable discharge. They thought he was crazy, but Marvin said that he had planned that whole thing. They would tell him to go out and cut the grass, and he would go out

82

and fall asleep. The sergeant would kick him and wake him up and put him in the brink. The next time they might put him on KP, and he would go to sleep there too. Whatever they told him to do he wouldn't do it."

Zeola said that she remembered when she was sixteen years old hearing the family discuss how somebody in the Air Force had all the soldiers write a letter as to why they liked or disliked being in that branch of the Air Force. Well, Marvin wrote about the terrible conditions and about the poor way things were handled. It turned out that Marvin's letter was so heavy that it reached all the way to the top, and they decided to let him go with an honorable discharge in order to get rid of him in 1957. Marvin was once quoted in an interview that the honorable discharge stated, *"Marvin Gay cannot adjust to regimentation and authority."* That doesn't say that he received an honorable discharge, but I am sure Zeola's statement is correct.

"When Marvin came home from the Air Force everybody was glad to see him. Even Father seemed glad that he was home," Zeola said.

Shortly after his returned in the late fifties Marvin started singing on the street corners, and then joined up with a singing group called the Marquees. When Marvin was nineteen years old apparently Harvey Fuqua from Harvey and the Moon Glows heard him singing and took him to Detroit and made him one of the Moon Glows. Zeola didn't dwell much on the late fifties because she was too young to know much about it. But she did mention that Marvin added the 'e' to his name during that time because he did not like to be connected with the word 'gay.' Later, Zeola began using the 'e' as well.

"I have been told that while Marvin was at a party in Detroit, Berry Gordy heard him singing at the piano and they had words. Not long after that he was signed as a single artist with Motown Records."

***

Zeola said that Marvin started taking drugs after he began recording in the studios.

"He said that he started doing cocaine because it helped him stay up during those late hours recording with Motown. He said that one night somebody came in with it, and the rest is history."

And what a short history it turned out to be. Instead of celebrating what should be a continuous release of new and wonderfully orchestrated songs from this fabulous musical genius of a man, we are continuously dealing with his senseless and untimely death.

Whenever Marvin would release a record Zeola said that she would wait to see what people would say.

"If they said it was good, I would say that he was my brother. He wasn't a star at that time. Those were the Motown years, of which I can't talk too much about because I wasn't traveling with Marvin then. But so many books and documentaries have been put out about Marvin and Motown that you've probably heard it all anyway. Marvin sent for me after he became a superstar and began touring the world."

After Marvin became a well-known celebrity the Gay family left the projects and moved to NW Washington DC. Zeola said that this was where Ebony Magazine came and did their spread on Marvin.

"Things were getting better and better financially, but things between my mother and father wasn't. Father was getting more and more jealous of Marvin because Marvin was doing more for Mom

than he was for Father. But what Father failed to realize was that Maw knew how to show love and appreciation. Father didn't."

Zeola said that she remembers when Marvin bought their mother a new Pontiac Bonneville. They were real popular then.

"My father tried to have a fit. So Marvin bought him a 1968 Cadillac. Father always had to be that one step above anybody else. I guess that kept him head of the household. But money breeds power and when Marvin became famous, and paid all the bills, he became the most powerful one in our household. He was now almost the head of our household, which caused Father to lose rank, and although Father continued to accept Marvin's gifts, he seemed to deeply resent everything about it."

Marvin started sending Alberta money so that she wouldn't have to do domestic cleaning anymore. Of course she shared it with Gay Sr., but Zeola said he didn't like the fact that Marvin sent the money to Alberta. He told her that he didn't want Marvin to send him anything with her name on it. He wanted his own separate money. So, Zeola said that her mother told Marvin and he got upset. She said that it made Marvin not to want to send his father anything, but in order to keep peace in the house, Zeola said that Marvin might send her mother $30,000 and he would send his father $10,000.

"I stayed home until 1973 and I worked every day of the week and my father took almost every dime I made for babysitting and rent. If I made $75 a week, my father took $60. The only time he ever let me keep a paycheck was at Christmas because he knew that I had to buy my kids presents. I didn't understand it, nor did I like it, but in a way he taught me to always pay my bills. Those things are instilled in me until this day. I don't like bills hanging over me. He was a firm believer that you have to pay for what you get."

85

Zeola remembered the time when Marvin came home and decided to buy her a car because he didn't like the fact that she had to catch the bus every day to go to work.

"When we got to the car dealership, Marvin had decided to buy me a Chevy Nova, but because I lived with Father, the dealership wanted some information from Father. I suppose that's the way they did things in those days. Maybe it was a racial thing, I don't know. All I remember was that they said that they needed information from my father because I lived with him. When Marvin called home to ask my father for his social security number, and whatever else he needed, my father asked him why he needed it. He asked Marvin what he was doing, and Marvin said that he was buying Sweetsie a car. My father told Marvin that he could not buy me a car because he was not going to give out his personal information to anybody. And that I didn't need a car. He said that I hung out too much already. Well, I cried and cried, and I cried some more. On the way home every time I saw a Nova pass me by I cried again. Marvin would say, 'Sweetsie, I'm so sorry.'"

Right after that Zeola said that she left her father's house and moved in with a girlfriend. At that time Marvin hadn't bought his father the Cadillac yet, so Zeola guessed that this had been another jealousy thing. She remembered her father saying, *"He's buying somebody else a new car and I don't even have one."* So Zeola felt that once again her father was just being mean and this time she was the recipient of his jealousies. She said that her father would say things like *"Is Marvin running things around here now?"*

I don't know if Zeola ever got the car because we never finished our conversation that day and of course I am unable to ask her now.

Zeola said that the tension between Marvin and her father got worse when Marvin became a real celebrity and made the hit song STUBBORN KIND OF FELLA.

"The Pentecostal church forced my father to resign from the church because in the Pentecostal religion at that time, singing rock and roll was against the principals of the church."

Gay Sr. was an Apostle Bishop and could not have a son singing that kind of music, according to Zeola.

"So, Father, who was one step from becoming Chief Apostle Priest of all the Pentecostal churches throughout the United States, had to put it all aside because of Marvin."

Zeola said that he would have been the big guy. He would have been the one who made all the decisions. He would have lived in the real big houses and got to make the rules for all the churches.

The very thought of this man making decisions for a church that I might attend frightened me silly. If I had been of the Pentecostal faith I am sure I would have changed religions almost immediately.

Everybody in the church and in the neighborhood still looked at Gay Sr. in a more respectful way because he had a son who was quickly becoming a superstar. Zeola said that he was still placed in a category above the others.

"But Father was still unhappy; especially when his best friend who was always in competition with him became that Apostle."

After Gay Sr. resigned from the church, Zeola said that the conflicts between him and Marvin got worse.

"I don't think Marvin ever realized the extent of what Father had given up because of him."

After that Zeola said that her father became a complete hermit.

"He started drinking more than ever. His attitude was unbearable. Marvin was quickly rising and Father was definitely falling. And the jealousies between the two of them were set for life. And Maw received the brunt of it all because Father took everything out on her. It seemed that if Maw so much as breathed wrong, Father would attack her with ridicule and humiliation."

***

Zeola said that she didn't think that Marvin started smoking weed until he had started his career and was married and living in Detroit.

"He didn't know it, but I was smoking weed too. He never wanted me to do anything wrong. He especially didn't want me to smoke marijuana. So whenever I would be around him and he was smoking he wouldn't offer me any. He didn't know that Frankie had already hooked me up with weed that he had brought home from Viet Nam. So when Marvin would come home or I would go to Detroit, he would give Frankie some, and I would be hiding in the basement saying, 'Frankie, come here! Don't put it out. Bring it back here and let me hit it!

Marvin always wanted to teach Zeola everything. He wouldn't have been happy if he thought somebody else taught her to smoke marijuana, so Zeola said that she let him think that she hadn't done it before.

"I remember one time in Detroit when I was in the car with Marvin and he decided to let me take a hit off his joint. So right after I did it, I started coughing, and he looked at me like I didn't know what I was doing. But what he didn't know was that I had been doing it for a long time, and that I always cough when I smoke weed. But that was important to him to be the first one."

But what Marvin did teach Zeola was how to get what she wanted without hurting people, she said. He told her to always be straightforward and honest.

88

"He said that you have to say what you want because if you don't say it, nobody will know what you want. I was very shy about saying what was on my mind. I would hold things back. He taught me not to do that. It's almost like the saying, 'Don't ask me a question if you're not ready for my answer because I am going to be truthful.'"

Zeola said that she will tell you how she feels and how she thinks it should be, and if you don't agree with it, then that's fine. But at least you know how she feels.

"The bottom line is to just be honest." She said adamantly.

This I understood completely because sometimes I have a problem being honest; especially if I think that it is going to hurt somebody's feelings. I think of it as protecting the situation. I don't think of it as lying, but in all reality a lie is a lie is a lie. However, I think I might prefer a liar to Gay Sr.

"I guess creativity is at its peak late at night because most artists record after midnight. That's how Marvin started taking cocaine. He said that it helped him stay up those late hours recording at the studios with Motown."

Marvin told Zeola that one night somebody came into the studio with cocaine, and the rest is history.

"Shortly after Marvin met Berry he met Berry's sister, Anna, and they got married. It wasn't long after Marvin's marriage to Anna that it became very rocky. Marvin told me that Anna was having an affair. He said that she liked young men, and Marvin told me that everybody in Detroit was talking about how she had bought cars and stuff for these guys. I didn't particularly care for Anna and her family at first because they didn't particularly care for us. They acted like they were superior to us because they had money and we didn't. And they had Marvin. Marvin became their property and their family. And they tried to keep him away from us. Other than that it didn't bother me. I think that if Marvin were happy marrying

a woman who was about seventeen years older than he was, I wouldn't have cared. That wasn't my business. "

Besides, Zeola said that age is just a number, and I agree with her. Sometimes she said that she thought Marvin was attracted to Anna because she reminded him of their mother.

"Besides being very close to Maw's age, she had some sweet ways like Maw. She pampered him and took care of him like my mom would have, and she was pretty, and she had money. I think Marvin was attracted to that."

Marvin told Zeola that Anna couldn't have children, so he made arrangements with Denise, Anna's niece, to have a baby for them. And she did. And according to Zeola that became Little Marvin III.

"I remember when Marvin said he was going to tell Little Marvin that he was adopted. Little Marvin was about 12 or 13 years old. My kids were up there when Marvin told him. They said that Little Marvin got really upset. I don't think he has ever gotten over that because he always seems so troubled. I love him very much, but I don't know how I can be of any help to him."

When Marvin had become a little well known and had made a couple of records in Detroit he would sometimes send for Zeola, but every time she visited them, she said that Anna would leave the house. And as long as she was in the house Zeola said that Anna would stay away.

"Marvin told me that when I would come to visit that Anna would say that she didn't want to be around me so that she could use that as an excuse to go and spend the night with other guys. But I never saw Anna with any other men. I still think that I was the main reason she left the house."

Zeola said that during that time she couldn't understand why the women in Marvin's life disliked her so much. But she says that she knows now.

"I think they just couldn't handle my relationship with Marvin. We were really close. And I think that maybe sometimes I might have deliberately made them jealous. I was young, and a little on the spoiled side. I don't think I did things to be mean though, and I can't think of a particular instance where I deliberately did something, but just looking back on my life, I'm sure I wasn't the perfect little sister at all times. I loved my brother very much, and could be possessive at times."

Zeola remembered one morning while visiting Marvin in Detroit, the man who worked for Anna and Marvin brought her breakfast in the guest room, and suddenly she said that she heard Anna hollering and screaming at him. She said that Anna yelled, *"You took her breakfast before you fed me? Are you out of your fucking mind?"* Zeola said that she cursed him out!

"I really felt so bad. I didn't want to be there after that."

Zeola said that Anna left town that day and didn't come back until after Zeola left Detroit.

"After that, every time I came to town she would leave. I guess that would be her excuse to go and hang out. And that's when she and Marvin started having problems. She didn't even like my mom. And anybody who didn't like Maw definitely must have something wrong with them because my mom was the most lovable person you would ever want to meet. Anna didn't seem to like anybody in the Gay family."

Once again I felt a slight contradiction because Zeola first said that Anna was sweet, and now she says that Anna didn't like the Gay family. So, I'm not quite clear on this last statement regarding Anna. Maybe Anna was sweet but still didn't like the Gay's. I think I could understand that probability because Gay Sr. did seem to leave little to be desired.

Zeola said Marvin always stayed friends with Anna. She said that he would always go up to Anna's house.

"I think they became better friends after the divorce than when they were together. And I contribute that to Anna's maturity and wealth. She knew how to handle herself. Unlike Jan, who went from rags to riches and didn't seem to appreciate anything, or know how to handle herself as a wife and mother."

Unfortunately, it wasn't until after Marvin's death that Zeola said that she and Anna decided to end the animosity.

"And we stuck to it. Even today, Anna and I are cool. Whenever we see each other we will hug and ask how the other has been. I love her."

***

According to Zeola, Gay Sr. did not like it at all when Marvin would come home to Washington DC and everybody, including the press, would come around the house.

"I think Father didn't like being around those people because they weren't there to see him. He still wanted to be the center of attention, and Marvin was slowly becoming 'the man'."

Nobody in the family treated Marvin special after he became a super star, Zeola commented.

"He didn't want to be treated any different. He just wanted to be Marvin. There was never any jealousy among any of us that I know of. The only jealousy came from Father, and he was seldom around."

Zeola said that her father didn't go to any of Marvin's concerts except the one at the Kennedy Center in Washington DC when Marvin performed WHAT'S GOING ON. According to her, the entire album was done there.

"I think Motown sent everybody out there who was on the album so that the concert would sound just like the album. I remember Marvin receiving the key to the city that time. It was the only event my father came to, and that really bothered Marvin

because he always invited Father to come wherever we went. Of course, Father was capable of coming to a show without telling anybody, and maybe standing somewhere in the back of the theatre where nobody could see him. I hope that there were times that he did that because I believe that he would have been impressed."

I never traveled with Marvin or had a one-on-one interview with him, but after listening to Zeola and reading about him, it is quite obvious to me that the lack of his father's love contributed heavily to his ill-timed death. I read once where he stated that all he ever wanted was for his father to throw his arms around him and tell him that he loved him and was proud of him. That seemed so sad to me because Marvin obviously allowed his emotional needs to control his life and ultimately destroy himself. I suppose that is a true trait of the gifted artist. Maybe without passion there would be no creation.

Zeola said that Marvin also had such a good heart.

"I remember once when he performed at the London Palladium the background singers were horrible. He said that they were all out of key, so he did the background over alone, and it turned out really great. He still gave them credit and he put their names on the album and everything. I don't want to say which song it was because he would not want me to do that. That's just how good he was about some things. I know that I have said it so many times, but my brother was a very special and loving person."

Zeola also thinks of Marvin as a humanitarian because she said that once while in New York, they were walking down the street and Marvin saw a homeless man who was cold and shivering. Without hesitation, Zeola said that Marvin pulled off his coat and gave it to the guy.

"He believed strongly in helping to improve the welfare of mankind. He wrote the song WHAT'S GOING ON because there was

so much unrest in the world at that time. Drugs were everywhere, Police were killing black children, and the whole world seemed at war."

Zeola remembered once Marvin had secretly admitted himself to a hospital to have his nose worked on because he had snorted so much cocaine that it had burned out all of the inner tissue. Before they left for the hospital, she said that Dick Gregory told Marvin that urine would heal the lining of his nose.

"He tried to get Marvin to put a drop of urine down his nose and Marvin didn't want to do it. I told Marvin that I wouldn't do it either, and we all joked about it."

The next morning Zeola said that they all met at the elevator and Marvin let out a big sigh of despair and said, *"You will never guess what I did."* She said that she knew immediately what he was talking about. She said to him, *"No you didn't."* And he said, *"Yes I did."* Marvin had put urine up his nose and told Zeola that it hurt his nose so bad that he thought he was going to die.

"Well, we all laughed until we cried. However, it was then that we realized just how serious Marvin was about not wanting to be hospitalized."

Zeola never told me whether or not it worked, but the fact that Marvin was trying to help himself was heart-warming. It was moments like this that made me love the spirit of this musical genius all the more.

Jeanne really got into the Jehovah's Witness religion, Zeola said.

"She had decided that Christmas was a pagan holiday, so it got down to none of us celebrating Christmas again. And my children became outraged. We had just come out here from Atlanta, and we were expecting to have this great Christmas, and Jeanne insisted that

we not celebrate. But Marvin didn't agree. He and Jeanne had a big argument about it. He told her that he couldn't understand why she would be so mean to the children. Finally, Marvin said that we could have Christmas at his house, and so we did. But Jean didn't allow her kids to come."

Zeola said that Marvin was like a little boy at Christmas. She said that he loved gifts, and he would put on everything that you gave him. If you gave him house shoes, she said that he would put them on. If you gave him pajamas, he would put them on. If you gave him a coat or a robe or a sweater, it didn't matter. He would put it all on. He was so funny because by the time the gift exchange was over, she said that he would be sitting there dressed in every piece of clothing that he got. And he would be telling all of us just how much he loved his gifts.

"It finally got to a point where you just didn't know what to get Marvin because he had everything. So I started getting him novelty stuff."

Even though Gay Sr. didn't participate in most of the things in the family's lives, he did participate in Christmas, according to Zeola.

"But he was so fucking picky that it wasn't funny. If you gave him a wallet and it wasn't real leather, or what he thought it should be, he would ask you "What is this?" Or, if the sweater wasn't cashmere, don't give it to him because he would hurt your feelings so bad. He only liked what he considered the good things in life."

I was amazed at the pride that I saw in Zeola's eyes when she talked about how her father preferred only the good things in life. I wanted to ask her if she realized that 'this man did not work.' But I am sure that it would not have done any good. It only helps me to understand all the more why Marvin was once quoted as saying that although he truly loved his family he sometimes resented having to take care of all of them.

***

Zeola said that Marvin didn't tell her that he was having financial trouble. She said that she found out about most of it from her mom, and she found out about the studio from Jeanne. *"She told me that the IRS would be sitting in the studio every day to make sure that no money was going out of there. Any money coming through there was taken."*

And even though her mom and her sister had told her the situation, the reality of Marvin's financial troubles didn't hit Zeola until she started working at his studio. She said that she didn't know for sure until she started answering the telephones and listening to some of Marvin's conversations to the IRS.

"And even then I wasn't worried because I agreed with Marvin about them wanting to take his money. I thought it was unfair too. I still think it's unfair."

Zeola gave an example of how she was feeling by telling the story about a young girl who didn't want to pay the government. She said that the girl asked who FICA was. It seems the girl didn't like the fact that she was giving her hard earned money to somebody she didn't know. Zeola explained to me that Marvin felt the same way, and did not want to pay the government the money owed.

"I will never forget how the government came in and took over Marvin's studio in Hollywood. It was really a bad time for Marvin. Under Chapter 13, these people are permitted to come in and sit and wait for anybody who comes in through the door with money, and they take it. This little short white man with thinning hair and glasses dressed in a suit sat out front on the sofa in front of me. He

96

didn't smile or talk to me or anything. He just took notes of who was coming and going out."

Zeola remembered that Jeanne had to book the studio in order to try and make money to pay the government people, and it wasn't like there was no business going on. A lot of money was being generated, and they were taking all of it.

The situation was pretty uncomfortable during those times, Zeola said. The studio stayed open 24 hours because most artists recorded late at night. And she said that those suited up government people stayed to collect every dime that was made.

"We all realized that they would probably take Marvin's house too, so Maw suggested that we go and get some stuff out of there. There's no use in letting them have everything he's got, she said. So we did it. We went to Hidden Hills and loaded up truck loads of everything we could. Jan didn't live in his house then, and Marvin was out of the state. He had left right after the government people came and sat in his studio. He couldn't handle it, and since he didn't have much money, he could only go as far as Hawaii."

Curtis Shaw was Marvin's lawyer at that time, and Zeola said that she always felt that he should have prevented this from happening.

"Curtis had a lot to do with helping Jeanne file for either chapter 11 or chapter 13, I don't remember. I just know that he handled a lot of Marvin's finances. I think he had the power of attorney too. Marvin really trusted Curtis. I think Curtis should have sat Marvin down and talked to him more about the consequences. Now, don't get me wrong, Marvin should have paid his taxes, and I'm not holding Curtis totally responsible for that. I just wish that he had tried to help Marvin more than it appears that he did."

Curtis Shaw made several statements to the press during that time about how he tried to convince Marvin to pay his taxes, but he said that Marvin would not listen.

Zeola said that she didn't know when Marvin stopped paying his taxes, but it had accumulated to over a million dollars. Regardless of that, she said that Marvin had the money. It was just that he was protesting.

"He didn't agree with the IRS so he just refused to pay the taxes. I guess you could say that this was just another form of Marvin's rebellion. Remember, he rebelled in the air force, he rebelled against Father and he rebelled against Berry. You name it and Marvin rebelled against it. Once again, it was that authority thing. Marvin looked at the IRS as trying to have complete authority over him and he wasn't going to allow it. That just wasn't going to happen."

Zeola said that she doesn't know a lot about Marvin while he was in Belgium, but she does know that he left this country because he felt that the system here wasn't fair. He started feeling this way when he wrote WHAT'S GOING ON.

"If you listen to the lyrics you can hear how he's talking about the system and paying taxes and stuff. He just felt that the government was wrong to tax us for working for our own money. If you win the lotto, why should they get half your money? And for what? What did they do to deserve it? To him they just had too much power. As I've said before, Marvin had a serious problem with authority. He knew that he owed a lot of money, and that they were on his ass, and there was nothing that he could do about it."

What's Going On
Marvin Gaye
(Al Cleveland/Marvin Gaye/Renaldo Benson)

Mother, mother
There's too many of you crying

98

Why did Marvin's Father Shoot and Kill Him?

Brother, brother, brother
There's far too many of you dying
You know we've got to find a way
To bring some lovin' here today - Ya

Father, father
We don't need to escalate
You see, war is not the answer
For only love can conquer hate
You know we've got to find a way
To bring some lovin' here today
Picket lines and picket signs
Don't punish me with brutality
Talk to me, so you can see
Oh, what's going on
What's going on
Ya, what's going on
Ah, what's going on
In the mean time
Right on, baby
Right on
Right on

Father, father, everybody thinks we're wrong
Oh, but who are they to judge us

Simply because our hair is long
Oh, you know we've got to find a way
To bring some understanding here today
Oh
Picket lines and picket signs
Don't punish me with brutality
Talk to me
So you can see
What's going on

> *Ya, what's going on*
> *Tell me what's going on*
> *I'll tell you what's going on - Uh*
> *Right on baby*
> *Right on baby*

I couldn't find anything in the lyrics of WHAT'S GOING ON pertaining to taxes, but I did remember Marvin talking about taxes in one of his songs, so out of curiosity, I began searching, and found that statement in the lyrics of INNER CITY BLUES MAKE ME WANNA HOLLER.

However, Marvin does emphasize his displeasure with the overall system as well as his distaste for the war in WHAT'S GOING ON.

Zeola remembered Marvin saying, *"Fuck it, I'm just not paying. I'll leave the country first."* And she says that he never did pay all of it. Supposedly, the promoters paid the rest for him.

"CBS paid some of it when they bought him out of Motown," Zeola said. *"They paid it so that he could come back into the country. Marvin was basically in exile."*

Zeola said that during that time artists weren't really into having their own CPA's. *"Their managers usually handled things. And you kind of trusted your managers, and didn't really check behind them."*

When Zeola heard that Marvin was coming home from Belgium she said that she got excited. She didn't care about the things that went on with Motown or anybody else. *"All that I knew was that Marvin was ready to come back, and that he was working on a record called SEXUAL HEALING. That's around the time CBS got involved. I'm not really sure how any of that worked either. The only thing I know about is that Larkin Arnold had to go to Belgium to get Marvin, and I was excited because I knew that if*

100

Marvin was on his way back, the party was on. I was so accustomed to Marvin being gone for long periods of time that I really didn't take Belgium too serious. All I was concerned with was that he was coming home and the good times would begin again. I think that kind of helps me to this day. Sometimes I pretend to myself that Marvin is just on another tour, and he will be coming home soon. That gets me through some bad times, that is, until reality sets in."

After that statement about reality setting in, I wanted so badly to explain to Zeola how reality should have set in a long time ago for Marvin's friends and family; long before Marvin went to Belgium; long before he died.

Reality should have set in when Marvin first began petitioning for peace of mind and unconditional love. But unfortunately his needs seem to have gone unnoticed. Nobody thought to listen. Nobody seemed to care. Everybody seems to have been so focused on their own personal gratification that they didn't appear to take the time to offer a little of themselves to help him unconditionally. Everything seems to have been based on what he could do for them.

Reality should have set in when he began to lose his studio. I have read many articles about how he refused to pay the government, but I've heard nothing regarding an outside source contacting him in an attempt to assist in his predicament. A proper business person might have been able to get through to him. I'm not saying that it would have been easy. I am just saying that nobody seemed to truly care enough to at least try and help this man without some sort of personal gains.

I have read about how some tried to get him to understand his tax situation and insisted that he would not listen. I am also aware of his paranoia and fears, but there had

101

to be someone out there capable of alleviating some of those anxieties, but the closest people seemed to be the most needy.

Reality should have set in when he was offered mounds and mounds of drugs instead of words of wisdom and encouragement. Instead, they used the drugs right along with him. Yes, I believe that many people tried to convince Marvin to turn his life around, but every time I read about somebody saying that, I read how some of the same people were doing the drugs right along with him. Even Zeola has made numerous statements about how Marvin said over and over that he just wanted peace, but even she interrupted it to mean that he want to die. How frustrating he must have felt to be surrounded by these people.

***

Zeola said that they used to go to Palm Springs every week because Marvin had been in detox and would go there for colonics. *"Marvin always thought that Palm Springs desert heat was a healing kind of heat as opposed to the heat in LA"* So she said that he rented a house in Palm Springs and they would drive down there periodically for relaxation.

"I will never forget the time we ran out of gas in Marvin's Rolls Royce. Marvin never carried money and the car was running out of gas, so Marvin searched thru car and found $2.50 in change which got us to Palm Springs. Marvin said that if we got behind a trailer truck the wind would pull the car and he was right. It was so crazy. We rode all the way to Palm Springs behind a big trailer truck. I couldn't believe that it worked. We made it there on fumes."

Zeola was on a roll that day. She seemed to enjoy telling great little stories about Marvin. And although they didn't tie anything together they showed how Marvin's mind worked at times.

"Marvin was very protective. He didn't like anybody I dated, especially a guy named Brian. He would tell me that he did not want Brian to stay at my house. Marvin leased me a beautiful convertible mustang. I loved that car. Marvin said that I could keep the car if I got rid of Brian. Well, I didn't get rid of him, so one morning Marvin called my house and Brian answered the phone, and about an hour later I saw somebody getting in my Mustang and driving off. Marvin had had the leasing company come and get the car. He told me that I could have the car back if I got rid of Brian."

I didn't get a chance to ask her if she gave up the car or gave up Brian.

***

Zeola often times described Marvin as the world's greatest procrastinator. She said that he would literally sit on the side of the bed in the morning for about twenty minutes just to collect himself. And then he would go in the bathroom and stay for about an hour. So if the plane left at 6 o'clock in the morning, she said that one can only imagine what time they had to start waking him up.

"The next morning when we would all get up because we had a plane to catch, somebody had to go in and wake Marvin up. And if the bodyguards couldn't get him up, they would always try to make me get him up but I told them that I wasn't going in there. Marvin was always too hateful in the morning."

Zeola also said that Marvin had a terrible fear of flying, so he would often times find any little thing to keep them from heading for the airport.

"There were many times when his procrastination would cause us to literally run through airports to catch our plane. And for some strange reason I think Marvin enjoyed that because if we missed a flight, which we did quite often, Marvin's theory was that we shouldn't have been on it in the first place. If the plane is still sitting

there when we arrive late, then Marvin would say that we should be on it."

Zeola said that she used to ride in first class all the time because Marvin wouldn't sit up there. *"He always said that the safest place in the plane was the tail end. He said that most people who survived plane crashes were sitting in the back of the plane. He explained that sometimes the tail end would break off from the other part of the plane when it crashed. I loved first class."*

Marvin's fear of flying took me back to my original point of view, which was if Marvin was so sure that he wanted to die, then why would he go through all of those motions to avoid getting killed in a plane crash? When I asked Zeola about it she only said that they were all on drugs, and she explained how paranoia played a big part of why Marvin was the way he was at that time. That explanation still did not satisfy me. I still fail to understand the logic. One ex-drug user later explained to me that there is no logic in that world. Maybe they are right.

One time Zeola said that they got on a flight and Marvin hated the way the pilot flew the plane. She said that he hated the way the pilot took off and he hated the way he landed. *"So when we stopped to pick up more passengers, we were supposed to stay in our seats, but Marvin made us all get up and get off the plane. When I think about it now it was so funny the way people watched us get off that plane knowing that we were not supposed to leave. It's almost like, if you see a whole group of people getting off a plane that you know are not suppose to leave, it makes you almost want to get off too. I know that if I saw that I would probably want to get up and get off too."*

Sometimes Zeola said that when they got to an airport Marvin would look at the flight and say, *"We're not getting on that plane."* So then they would be running late for the show, so he would hire a limo to take them the rest of the way. She said that he always relied on his second sense.

"Every time we got a plane to Atlanta it seemed like something strange happened on that plane. So I would always know ahead of time that we were in for another adventure in the sky. But it didn't bother me because I had my comfortable first class seat and any drink that I wanted."

CHAPTER
8

SEDUCTION

Back in the 70's in Washington DC if you moved up to the
North West it meant that your status had changed. It meant
that you were now middle class and Marvin had moved the
Gay family up near 16th street. Zeola said that in those days
all the rich people lived on 16th street and up. And she
remembered an incident during that time when Gay Sr. finally
acted like what she perceived a real father might be.

*"The higher you go, the more important you are so we were
almost there. I was about twenty four years old and had met some
friends up there, and every time we went somewhere people would
say something about this person named Iola. Their conversations
would be about Iola this and Iola that. They would say that this Iola
had a body like a brick house, and they would say how bad she was.
They said that she made love to women as good as she did men.
Everybody loved Iola. They told me how they all went to someplace
called Brandywine and they ran off the road and shit because Iola
was giving somebody head and shit. Everybody called Iola 'the
teacher.' They all said that what she had was like gold and that she
was very picky. She didn't squander herself to anybody who wasn't
worthy of it because what she had was gold. So I was sitting there
wondering what this girl looked like with a name like mine."*

Zeola smiled when I asked her what happened when she
finally met Iola. She quickly emphasized how young and wild
they were in those days. *"I hope that by telling this story Iola
won't be mad at me because she is a happily married woman now,
but I've got to give it up."*

Zeola said that she and her best friend Gloria were kicking
it in D.C. with the Red Skins. She said that they were dating a
couple of the players. Zeola said that she had gone to this
party and everybody was in the back room smoking weed and
getting high.

"Weed was all we did then."

Zeola described her outfit to me. She said that she had on a sexy pink fishnet dress with lots of holes in it. You could see her skin through the holes so she said that she wore a little purple leotard underneath. She said that if Marvin had not seen her in this type of clothing, and he would have probably not approved, but she was a woman now, so it didn't really matter.

"I thought I was bad. I was small and shapely, and you couldn't tell me shit. I thought I had it going on." She said with that mischievous 'Marvin' smile.

A weed room had been set aside at the party for those wanting to smoke marijuana. Zeola described how there were a lot of people sitting around in a dark smoky room getting high on weed. She said that while she was sitting on the bed in that room next to her friend Gloria, she could feel some eyes on her. She said that she knew that somebody was watching her. Finally, she realized that a woman in the corner was staring at her. She said that the woman had a look on her face that she could not describe.

Zeola had already said that the woman did both men and women, so I asked her if it was a look of a man flirting with her, and she said, *"No."* She said that the woman was so feminine and beautiful that it was unbelievable. Zeola said that she didn't come across as a lesbian or a dyke. She said that the looks were more sensual. *"I would look over at the girl once in a while and the girl would still be looking at me so I finally said, 'Hi' to her because she was beginning to make me feel uncomfortable. She spoke and told me that I looked very nice so I said, 'Thank you.'"*

Zeola said her name, and then she asked the girl the same thing and the girl said that her name was Iola.

When Iola asked for her phone number, Zeola said that she gave it to her willingly and then left the party. On the way home she and Gloria talked about the incident. She said that although she was nervous and apprehensive about what went down, she was curious about this Iola. She said that she wondered why this woman approached her.

When I later started writing this chapter I went back over my notes and audio tapes to see if Zeola had given me a better description of Iola, but I couldn't find anything about her other than the fact that she was a Black woman with soft smooth skin, great figure and sensuous eyes. I think maybe we didn't get into more of her description because Zeola kept reminiscing about how good it felt that her father finally came to her rescue from this woman. I had no idea what she was talking about because she never finished her sentence, yet I knew not to interrupt her because she would get so totally off-track and we would never get back to how Iola got with Marvin.

Zeola said that the next day, which was a Sunday, the telephone rang and it was Iola calling to invite her to dinner. When Zeola got to Iola's house she said that she was totally amazed because her house was so well decorated.

"Iola fixed spaghetti, and had everything laid out. She had the checkered table cloth, garlic bread and the perfect wine. And then she had the best weed ever."

Sometimes Zeola could be quite funny, and this was one of those times. She said that I had to understand that she was sort of young, and had just come out of the projects and wasn't used to all of this. She explained that the little bit of weed that she had smoked was usually at somebody's house or out of somebody's car or something, so all of this was amazing to her. She said that the house was calm and relaxing and beautiful. Not at all like Gay Sr.'s house.

Zeola said that they talked about music and lots of other things and realized that they had so much in common, plus, she said that the food was excellent.

Zeola said that she and Iola instantly formed a bond. She said that Iola recognized that she was sort of green and didn't know very much about a lot of things. *"But Iola seemed well versed on many things, and I liked that."*

Iola was about five years older than Zeola.

The following weekend Zeola said that Redskins were playing ball in Virginia and she was invited to a party there. *"We were all smoking and getting high and switching partners and shit but even though I was having fun I didn't have any orgasms because that was something that always seemed hard for me to do. I always needed something special for that. The mood had to be right; music, candles and foreplay, the whole bit."*

All the while she was telling me this story I was watching her to see her reactions because I could not imagine me telling anybody something so personal, especially knowing that it was about to be written up in a book. It just would have been very embarrassing for me, but Zeola was cool and calm. It was just another part of her experiences, and she "had to give it up."

"When she made love to me, it was great."

After that, Zeola said that they started spending a lot of time together. She said that Iola showed her things about sex that she never knew was possible. Zeola really seemed to admire Iola.

"Iola had a sculptured ass and a tiny little waistline. She had perfect boobs, and she could do everything. She could fix a car, change a tire, grow shit in a garden, and she could paint. She was

110

like an interior decorator. You name it and Iola could do it. And sexually she had it going on."

Zeola said after kicking it with Iola for a few months she took Iola to Detroit to meet Marvin. However, she said that she never told him about anything dealing with the Iola and her because she did not know how Marvin would react. He was so protective of his little sister even though he was now living in another state.

"Marvin and Anna were having some problems. Anna was being shitty, and Marvin was unhappy, so I thought Iola could make Marvin happy because I knew that she was excellent in bed. She had taught me so much about sex. I thought of her as my teacher. She taught me how to make love to men".

Zeola said that she loved making a man feel good, but she said that it was not the same with a woman. She only did it because she felt compelled to return the favors to Iola. She offered great tips on how to sex a man, but I didn't think it was appropriate for this book.

"Marvin liked Iola. They hit it off really well. And Marvin never mentioned to me anything about whether Iola and I had anything going on, but he probably knew. He was smart."

Eventually Zeola said that people started talking about Iola and her because they were hanging out too much. But she said that she wasn't feeling bad about it because she knew that she loved men.

"Iola was nice and all, but I liked men, and that's all there was to it. This just didn't feel complete for me. There was no question about it. I liked dick."

That summer Zeola said that she and Iola had decided to get a house and move in together. She said that the house even had a room for her kids. During this time Zeola said that she

111

didn't think that her parents knew anything about her relationship with Iola or her lifestyle.

Before making the big move, Zeola said that she was outside walking home in the rain and she started crying because something was not right in her life. She said that she liked walking in the rain in Washington DC because it felt good on her skin when the weather was real hot. By the time she got home she said that she looked up and her father was sitting in the window as usual and he saw her coming down the street crying so he came down stairs to meet her at the door and asked her what was wrong. Zeola said that her father seemed to know what had been going on because for the first time he acted like a father and held her while she cried, and then he told her that she didn't have to do anything that she didn't want to do.

I did not expect Zeola to tell me that Gay Sr. responded to her in that manner. As soon as she mentioned that he was looking out of his window and proceeded downstairs to greet her, my imagination had immediately led me to envisioning this eccentric and effeminate man racing down this huge GONE WITH THE WIND type staircase in his silk robe, wearing a woman's wig and stockings, and telling her to go for it with Iola. Instead, she described him as a compassionate and caring father-like figure offering her good solid advice. So I suppose it is true that there is a little good in all of us, which is what Zeola has been trying to say all along.

So her next step was to tell Iola that she was not going to move in with her, and when she did tell her she said that Iola was cool with it. Zeola said that they didn't have sex anymore after that, but they did remain friends. And even today, they might talk on the telephone every few years, but the conversations never go back to their involvement with each other, but more about their love for Marvin.

***

Shortly after that Zeola said that she got involved with Smokey.

"I remember one time when I was coming home from Detroit with Marvin and his friends and the car was really crowded and I had to sit on Smokey's lap and when I got home I thought about the fact that I had actually sat on Smokey's lap. But then it just left my mind. Later I went to see Smokey in a concert and I wore a dress that had holes all the way down each side past my butt, so you couldn't wear anything underneath it; no stockings or anything because you could see your whole body. And when I went back stage to say hi to Smokey and then left out I heard him say, 'Damn!' That was the first time I think he had seen me as a woman. I wasn't just Marvin's little sister."

Zeola said that when she went home she told her mother about it. "I used to tell Maw everything." Well, Alberta just happened to mention it to Marvin, and Zeola said that Marvin went to Smokey because they hung out together. She said they were like best friends. So Marvin told Smokey that he can't fuck with his baby sister.

"Smokey said that Marvin told him that if he ever fucked me the relationship between them would be over."

Zeola said that the next time she and Smokey were together they did a lot of heavy kissing and stuff, but they never had intercourse because Smokey would say, *"I can't do it. I can't do it. I keep hearing Marvin's words."* But she wanted him so she would say, *"I'm not going to tell him."* But Smokey wouldn't do it. He just said, *"I can't. Even though you wouldn't tell him, I would know. I love Gaye"*

Zeola said that she respected him for that, but there was this thing inside her that still wanted to break him. She said, *"I'm a Gay. I wanted to break him."* She said that she tried her best to persuade him. *"You're going to listen to Marvin?"* She asked. But he wouldn't do it.

A few years past and Zeola was living in Atlanta and Smokey came to Atlanta with Marvin. She said that she hadn't seen Smokey in a long time, and she had been telling everybody that Smokey was her man. She said that she called him up at the hotel to let him know that she was in town and he invited her down to the hotel. Finally, they were going to finally get together, but she said that it was the last day of her period. She said she was so upset because this was her chance to finally break him. She said that when she got to his room she and Smokey started making out on the bed, and he was just about ready to penetrate and she stopped it. She said that she played it off and told him that she had to get back to work, and she would see him later. The real problem was that she didn't want to have to go to the bathroom and remove her tampon and deal with anything else that might have occurred as a result of her menstruating. *"I just didn't want to deal with all that."*

The relationship ended after that. Zeola said that she and Smokey never got together again. However, she confessed that even after all that, one of the main reasons she wanted to move to California was because she wanted to see Smokey again. She said that he and Marvin remained friends all the way up to when Marvin went to Europe after the IRS and Motown issues.

"I can't remember the year, but I am sure that Smokey remembers. Marvin wasn't doing well. He had started doing drugs a lot, and had gone to Hawaii and told me that he was living on the

beach in a little ice cream truck. He said that he had called Smokey and asked if he would send him some money so that he could go to a hotel, but Smokey wouldn't send him the money because he claimed that Marvin would have bought drugs with it. Marvin told me that he was truly truly hurt over that. He was down and out and said that he just couldn't believe that he called on his best friend and he wouldn't give him the money regardless of what he would do with it. For all Smokey knew, Marvin might have been in rehab or something trying to kick the habit. Marvin felt that Smokey didn't know what the situation was. So that sort of started me to thinking differently about Smokey."

According to Zeola, Marvin stayed mad with Smokey for a long time. Later Smokey apologized and Marvin forgave him, but she said that they never really became close again. She said that even when she had contact with Smokey at the funeral she still did not feel the same about him.

After listening to Zeola, I could understand Marvin's reasoning for the friendship not remaining the same, but at the same time I admire Smokey for not becoming an enabler to Marvin's drug addiction.

CHAPTER
9

LORENA

Zeola started smoking weed and doing cocaine in the early 70's. She said that she was still living with her parents in D.C. She said that once she started traveling with Marvin, she loved cocaine because it kept her small, but as a result of the abuse, she now suffers with insomnia.

"We all needed it on tour because we kept crazy hours. By the time we left a venue it would be about one or two o'clock in the morning and then we might go back to the hotel and eat something because we would all be hungry by then. Then we might smoke some weed, and then maybe snort some more cocaine, and then we might not be hungry anymore."

Zeola said that they might get about two hours of sleep and then it was time to hop on another airplane.

"Everybody in the 60's and 70's were either taking drugs or selling them. And the heavy drug of that time was Heroin. Cocaine was just a social drug. If you would go to a social event there was always a special room that you would go into and take a couple of hits and then party. "

According to Zeola, nobody in her family knew that she was doing cocaine.

"I didn't like cocaine at first. I couldn't understand what anybody could see in it. The drain was awful. It was so bitter."

Zeola explained that the drain is when you snort cocaine, and as it enters your system you get a drain like your nose is running. But it drains backwards instead of forward. It is similar to having a cold and your nose is running down your lip, except she said that it drains backwards, and you can taste the bitterness.

"And then there's the freeze. I didn't like that either. It numbs the inside of your mouth and lips as you swallow the drain that's

117

going down the back of your throat. I didn't like that at all. But the more I did it the more I got used to the drain."

She said that she started out doing little tiny hits. *"But one day I realized that I was beginning to like it because I started taking bigger hits. What I liked about it was the energy it gave me. And it helped me think. But it didn't make me horny like it does for a lot of people. But it did help me get into it quicker. What I liked more than anything else was that I didn't eat. It kept me small."*

Back in the day Zeola said that they used tiny little spoons to snort cocaine. Some people wore them around their necks on chains. And even though she started using the stuff, she said that she wouldn't dare be caught with one of those spoons or anything else that indicated drugs.

"Father would have been worst than any jail I could ever imagined, so most of the time I did the baby fingernail thing. A lot of people used their baby fingernail to pick up the cocaine, so that's what I did."

Zeola claimed that she wasn't hooked on it or anything like that. She said that she didn't do it as much as everybody else.

"Weed was more important to my friends and me. We did mescaline once in a while, but I didn't like hallucinating. I don't think Marvin ever tried anything like that. I'm sure he would have told me if he had because we talked about everything."

It used to take forever for Marvin to get up and get dressed in the morning. Zeola said that was because he would be up all night. She said that cocaine played the big factor in that, especially during that last tour.

"It was amazing that no matter what town we went to, it could be any hick town, but when we got there the cocaine would be waiting for us. The bellman might tell Marvin or his body guard,

Andre, where it was, or who to go see, and then he would send me and Robin to go and get it."

Zeola said that one day she and Robin had to go to the laundry room in the back of the hotel.

"We were so scared because we were thinking all kinds of shit, like this looked like where they kill people and shit. We thought that once we got the drugs we would get busted and stuff. But we found out later that the promoters were responsible for supplying the drugs so nothing would have happened to us."

All the while Zeola was talking and I was writing I could think of nothing except how unfortunate it is that so many entertainers fall into the drug trap. Promoters must have a field day filling them with drugs so that they can rake in the money. What a waste of life. And out of all of those people surrounding Marvin, nobody seemed to have the brains to help him get his life in order. Instead, it looks like they were all there smoking and doing blow right along with him. Nobody seemed to have attempted to help him during that time. However, his brother Frankie as well as his friend, Dick Gregory, has both been overheard at one time or another trying to explain to Marvin why he should stop taking the drugs.

***

A Puerto Rican attorney told Zeola once that Columbians come over here with cocaine and they establish stores, like vacuum cleaner places or sewing machine places and they distribute the drugs out of the stores. The stores, according to Zeola, are generally located in the Black communities. However, only a few Blacks are trusted to operate the business. And she said that all of this was operated by 'The General.'

"Columbians who are dirt poor, who literally have nothing are brought over here to work in these places. They tell them that if they get busted in America their families will be taken care of so they are eager to do it."

Zeola said that this type of cocaine is called Lorena. She said that it is considered some of the best cocaine in the world.

"When the cocaine comes here, it comes in packets. Lorens translates into beautiful flower. And it is believed to be the best cocaine that you can get anywhere. It has the capacity to be stepped on eight times, which means that you can add to it at least eight times before selling it."

She said that another term would be to 'cut' it eight times. The money that she said that the General makes for distributing Columbian to the whole Black community is mind-boggling because he can step on it as many as five or six more times and then you can step on it a few more times before it hits the streets.

"You could always tell the Lorena because it was rainbow in color. It looked like fish scales. It was beautiful, if you can call such a deviate drug beautiful."

I asked Zeola to clarify the fact that this sounded as if this was not a drug that the average person would put up their nose in its original state.

"Some people might be able to hit it once, but it is a rare person who could handle it without some sort of immediate damage to the nose. Generally, you would immediately end up with a raw nose and watering eyes."

Zeola had mentioned something about a man they called the General. She said that he was the head of this Columbian cartel.

"My friend, Robin and I always wanted to meet The General, but Marvin would never let us meet him."

CHAPTER
10

THE APPROVAL

Some days when I picked Zeola up for our sessions she would appear to be a little stressed or agitated. Most of the time she stressed that it was over money. She never seemed to have very much of it. She had a part-time job, but often times I suspect she depended on government assistance to get by. It was just so hard for me to imagine her being in such financial need when Marvin's music is still being played daily in almost every modern household in America, both on the radio daily and television. And one can only imagine what the European market must be like. When I went on-line to check it out, I found more of his music available in countries such as Belgium and England than I found in the good ole United States of America.

One day I asked Zeola where all that money was going and she explained that Marvin's ex-wife, Jan, is in control of a lot of it. I asked her how that could be when they were divorced before Marvin died. She explained that the children are the recipients, and the ex-wife is the executer of their holdings. I then asked Zeola why she wasn't given a little something now and then, and she explained that she and Jan were not on good terms. Zeola told me that she had not talked to Jan in years. She said Jan did not like her, and that Jan looked down on her for some reason.

Often times now I wonder how that relationship is going between the two of them now that Zeola has been paid to stop her story.

I asked Zeola about her relationship between Nona and Frankie, Marvin's children. I knew that Nona was quickly becoming a famous actress, but I knew very little about Marvin's two sons. I only knew that Marvin had a son prior to his marriage to Jan, and another son by Jan. Zeola said that the kids had never disrespected her, but were seldom brought

122

around her and her children. I could tell that this conversation did not set well with her, so I didn't ask anymore questions about Marvin's offspring at that time. I had learned by now that when Zeola did not want to discuss something that I should let it go for the moment, which I did.

The movie that I had been working on when I met Zeola turned out to be a big hoax. I had been on the job for one month and still had not gotten paid. Because of years of experience as a producer, it did not take long to figure out that the production company had no money. They were working on false hopes and dreams like a lot of Hollywood folks, and they were not able to pay most of us so I was forced to part with that assignment. Thus, leaving me short a month's pay.

Soon after that I was offered new employment but I had already committed myself to Zeola. So the fuel that I used a pick her up each day, as well as the food and wine that I so generously supplied was taking its toll on my little budget, so I wasn't about to blow this session over one curiosity about Jan's kids or Marvin's older son. Besides, this was finally turning out to be a good day. Zeola seemed to have set aside her financial woes for the moment, and we continued the session laughing and reminiscing about Zeola's past with Marvin and her seemingly dysfunctional family.

Zeola smiled as she looked over the hors devours that I had placed on the tray before her. Usually I would prepare a pasta dish or something more filling, but I wasn't able to do it this time. I didn't have the money to buy all of the proper ingredients. My savings was quickly dwindling. So, earlier that day I had reached into my freezer and pulled out a quart size Tupper Ware container of already prepared frozen pastries that were left over from an informal gathering that I had had the week before. I heated them in the microwave oven, carefully placed them on a dinner size plate and brought them out on my favorite yellow wooden food tray.

"Thank you." Zeola said with a pleasant smile.

I always considered her a great guest because she never complained about any of the food that I prepared for her.

While the two of us politely devoured a few of the tasty quiche tidbits, I poured us both a glass of red Merlot wine. Once again, Zeola seemed pleased and thanked me. The hot hors devours worked well with the wine. After that, Zeola meticulously opened her huge purse and reached in to pull out what I had previously named 'her medicine.'

I was always amazed at how she seemed to know just where to find her stash in that big black bag. But she went right to it again. While she was retrieving her paraphernalia from her purse, I went to my office to get my special 'Marvin' note pad, a ball point pen and the tape recorder. By the time I got back Zeola had lit up her first marijuana joint of the session and was ready to talk, so I turned on the tape recorder, and we went to work.

"We attended church on Saturdays, and it seemed that every time we got ready to pile in the car, nobody could find Marvin. Somehow he would just get lost. Father would get so mad because Marvin was nowhere to be found. And by the time we did find him, he would be somewhere gazing up at the sky or looking at some rocks or staring at some birds. He was only about twelve years old and he already had developed a passion for God's creations. Sometimes he would actually be out there singing to the birds."

Whenever Zeola spoke about her childhood with Marvin, her eyes lit up, and she became a different person. Energy seemed to flow through her body as she took her last hit and then put out her joint and sat back and relaxed. Those were the times when I truly enjoyed her company. We would laugh one moment and then get teary-eyed the next.

"Marvin truly was a musical genius!" Zeola blurted out just before brushing tiny bits of crumbs from her lap. I could tell that she seemed genuinely proud of being the sister of such a famous man. She even gives parties at local venues in and around Los Angeles California on behalf of Marvin's birthday, which was April 2nd. However, I sometimes question the true motives behind the festivities. Instead of a celebration for Marvin, it seemed to me on my first invite that most of it was about nothing more than a bunch of people attempting to recapture the old days on behalf of themselves.

Before Zeola arrived I saw a couple on the dance floor who appeared to have dressed like the 70's and was doing all the old moves while dancing to Marvin's songs. It reminded me of "Blues Nights" in Long Beach California when everybody shows up at Blues events with their old St. Louis type broke-down flashy hats with the colorful satin shirts, platform shoes and bell bottom pants. It was great to see the love for Marvin, but at the same time I was somewhat saddened by such a strong need for a fabrication of the past. Their mannerisms and slang along with the strong smell of weed seemed to put them in a place that I could not relate.

It is one thing to celebrate a loved one who has passed on, and to have fun doing it, and I am probably at the top of the list when it comes to enjoying Marvin's music, but this night seemed different somehow. Dressing like the 70's in order to make the party more fun-like seemed like a fun thing, but that was not the part that was troubling me. I overheard a small group of individuals, most who were over fifty years old and out of work, talking about the past. It was then that I realized that they were still holding on to the belief that they are going

125

to someday be called again to work for a new musical icon yet to come along. When, in fact, this particular group of folks were too old and worn out to be hired by anybody. Hollywood has a reputation of dismissing most production people over the age of about 35 years mostly because they are always looking for new ideas as well as wanting to hire people who posses the necessary energy to keep the pace. So the thought of somebody bringing these folks aboard seemed somewhat hopeless to me. But who am I to judge? Maybe hope is what they need. Maybe reminiscing is a good thing for some people. After thinking about it for a few hours while waiting for Zeola to appear, I came to accept the fact that maybe I was the one who was out of place. These people have chosen to live in the past for whatever the reason, and if that is what makes them happy and keeps them going, then more power to them. I suppose it is easier for some to relive the good ole days, rather than focus on what is at hand or what might lie ahead.

And what a great past they must have had with the big long limousines, wild parties, drugs and the support of this handsome and sexy musical icon. That's when I almost became envious of them. At least they have an interesting past to hold on to. And if that's what holds them together, so be it.

Even though Marvin's birthday party was radioed to begin at 9:00 p.m., hosted by Zeola, she showed up close to midnight with an entourage of friends and family surrounding her as if she was Marvin himself making a grandiose entrance with the expectancy of a multitude of screaming fans and paparazzi. But of course, that did not happen.

Dressed in sexy attire and spiked high heels, her daughters and girlfriends all had the persona of overly enthusiastic groupies sauntering through the lobby, desperate for attention and smelling like they had just been released from a week long stay in a room filled with freshly lit marijuana. Once again I was back to my original feelings about this event because my heart sank as I watched this lovely lady desperately attempting to relive the past.

Although nicely dressed in her new sheer polyester outfit, Zeola was acting like a wannabe super star wreaking of weed and greeting people with the sincerity of a queen to her court.

"Have I missed something here?" I asked myself. *"Did these people's lives literally cease to exist at the loss of Marvin? Are their spirits so truly broken that this is all they have left to live for – a moment of grandeur on Marvin's behalf?"*

Suddenly I became overwhelmed with compassion. I thought, *"If Marvin could only see the enormity of the effect that he has had on his family and fans, surely he would return here and tell them all to get on with their lives."*

Maybe he has already done that, and they just aren't listening, I thought to myself. He must have tried to communicate with somebody because his spiritual communiqué with me is sometimes overwhelming, and I barely knew him. Maybe they aren't tuned in to the right channel spiritually.

I am aware that some religions teach the belief that once you die your spirit is gone and will not return until Christ comes back. And until that time, all spirits revisited are not of God's will. But my Christian church teaches something different. It is my Christian belief that when we die our physical bodies are gone, but our spirits live on through Christ. I believe in angels and messages from the Almighty. And I believe that an angelic spirit is leading me to finish this story. I strongly feel that Marvin wants closure, and this is

127

how I have been directed. I know that angels surround my life, and my spiritual encounters regarding Marvin are real.

I believe with all my heart that even though Marvin lived a portion of his life in such a way that some might not approve, he was still truly one of God's special people, and even though he might be gone in the flesh, his spirit lives on. I believe that only someone with the true power of the Holy Spirit could create such beautiful music and spread so much peace and love around the world. No doubt about it, Marvin was a blessing. And no doubt about it, I feel blessed to have the opportunity to write his story. I say that it is his story because I believe that in some way he chose me to write it and Zeola to tell it to me. She has mentioned several times to me how disappointed Marvin was in the David Ritz story, so maybe this is the story he wants revealed.

***

It was about 8:30 on a Saturday morning, and normally I would be sitting at my desk upstairs in my office working, but after having a very satisfying breakfast of wheat toast, scrambled eggs and coffee, I noticed how bright the sun was shining through my kitchen window off the patio, so I decided to go and get my laptop computer and tape recorder and work downstairs at the kitchen table.

My work went well that morning. I had listened to several of Zeola's tapes, and concluded that I had a long road ahead of me with this story because the turmoil and heartache that Marvin seemed to have suffered was heart-wrenching. I began to realize that being a super star was definitely not what it was cut out to be.

Convinced that I had explained my spiritual beliefs the best that I could without disrespecting other religions or beliefs, I sat back in my chair and thought about what I had just listened to on the tapes as well as what I had written about Marvin's grief with his family and ex-wife. And for whatever the reason, I really felt the need for some sort of confirmation. I don't know why, and I wasn't sure who I needed to hear it from; I just, at that moment, wanted somebody to tell me that it was okay to write this devastating story about this troubled individual.

It had rained the night before so the sky was clear enough to see the mountains in the distance. I thought how unusual that was for the Los Angeles area because we have so much smog that generally one can't even see the big Hollywood sign from where I live. But this day was absolutely gorgeous, so I just sat there staring up at the clear blue sky and the fluffy white clouds.

After sitting there a while and looking out at the sky, and thinking about what Zeola had said about Marvin always looking up at the sky and how much he loved all of God's little creatures, I suddenly realized that it was Marvin's approval that I wanted.

Only moments later, out of the corner of my eye, I saw something quietly fluttering about outside on my patio, and when I turned to look, to my surprise, it was a beautiful gray dove perched itself on the white balcony chair nearest my glass patio door. At first I was a bit startled because I had never seen a dove on my patio before. There had been an occasional incident with bees and wasps, and sometimes a hummingbird or two buzzing around my flowers, and depending on the time of year, crows and pigeons fly about the neighborhood, but this was an unusual occurrence for me.

I just sat there for a moment and stared at the interesting bird, and it seemed as if it was, in turn, looking at me. And then I suddenly felt a surge of warmth and excitement race throughout my body. I knew immediately that this was the confirmation that I was waiting for. And as soon as I smiled and thanked the little bird for its approval, it was gone, and I have never seen it since. What a wonderful moment that was. And little did I know that there would be many more incidents like it throughout this project.

I have always had a special ability that I cannot explain. Some call it super natural powers, while others might call it a spiritual connection. Scientists have named it psychic powers. I call it "Angels Revisited."

I will never forget the time when one of my Christian friends tried to convince me that my abilities were that of the devil. Another person did not say that it was from the devil but tried to convince me that the bible says that we must not communicate with the spirit world. Therefore, they contended that their belief is that this ability is not of God's choosing. But once I reminded them of the existence of God's angels, and provided them with the proper literature, I have not heard another negative word from any of them.

Although I sometimes have premonitions or receive messages from what seems to be the "other side" I know that I am a child of God, and that anything that passes through me is of God's doing.

CHAPTER
11

JAN

"If Marvin had never met Jan, Marvin would still be alive today." Zeola stated adamantly.

Having not heard from Jan in years, Zeola said that she was surprised to hear Jan's voice on her answer machine requesting to meet with her.

Zeola said that she knew that Jan was coming to ask for something because she would not have called otherwise. She said that she doesn't hate Jan, but she doesn't like her very much.

When Jan arrived at her home, Zeola said that she requested the video tape of Mohammad Ali and Marvin sparing together because she said that MTV wanted to do a special on Marvin. Zeola said that she did not have the tape, but referred Jan to someone else.

Before Jan left that day, Zeola said that she did not understand why Jan and Jan's family had distanced themselves from her and her family, so she asked Jan about it. Jan explained to her that she had been upset because Zeola had sold a painting of Marvin to Eddie Murphy and had not given her and her kids part of the money.

"Mind you, this was my painting, and my family got nothing from Marvin's estate. But Jan and her kids and Little Marvin get everything from the estate."

Zeola said that she doesn't have a problem with them getting everything because Marvin didn't leave a Will so that's how it worked itself out. Little Marvin turned eighteen years old that year so the estate went to him and Jan's children.

"I thought that this was so selfish of Jan because my family had been dealing with my mother's cancer, and she had no insurance and we didn't have the kind of money to give her the kind of help she

132

needed. This was a big strain on all of us. My family had been dealing with a lot, so I didn't like her reasons."

After that Zeola said that Jan then asked her why she didn't like her, and Zeola said, *"I've been upset with you ever since you tried to kill Marvin."* Zeola said that Jan asked her what she was talking about, and Zeola reminded her of the time that she had given Zeola the poison for Marvin, but Jan denied it. Zeola said that Jan did not acknowledge that she gave her poison.

Finally, I thought, I might get the answers to Zeola's poisoning allegation. Although I had not brought it up, I had not forgotten the serious allegation.

Zeola started by explaining to me that Marvin had become a big handful because a lot of the responsibilities had fallen on her. She said that she had to watch his back and make sure that things were cool around other people. *"I was like his right hand."*

This got to be too much for Zeola so she said that she sent for her girlfriend, Robin, who met up with them in Atlanta, Georgia. Zeola said that Marvin liked Robin so it was no problem having her there.

"Marvin wouldn't allow anybody to give him food or drink except me. So just before each show I would prepare for him a special blended drink of parsley, bananas and apple juice along with a hand full of vitamins that I would get from Dick Gregory, plus a vitamin B12 shot."

After that, Zeola said that she would prepare another concoction of Cheyenne pepper, lemon and honey. Zeola said that first, Jan would give her a spoon full of alum to give to Marvin, which he would swallow followed by the parsley, banana and apple juice. And then he would take the concoction of Cheyenne pepper, lemon and honey, and go on stage.

By the time they got to the Boston tour, Zeola said that she had given Marvin approximately four jars of this alum before it dawned on her that she didn't know what alum was. She said that she never really took notice of anything wrong until she actually saw the jar, which was covered by a brown paper bag. She said that the paper bag is what prompted her to ask questions.

"It was really stupid of me not to question this before, but I was having too much fun. I was loaded half the time. Apparently Jan must have told Marvin that it was good for him because he knew that I was giving him something that was coming from Jan."

After discussing it with her friend Robin, they decided to read the back of the jar, and it said something about it containing alum which is sometimes used in a douche bag. She said that they took the jar to a local pharmacist who told them that the douche powder was something that prostitutes put in their douche to tighten up their pussy because they have sex all the time and they have to keep it tight. She said that they don't want their pussy to be so that a truck could go in 'em.

"Then I started reading the back of the jar again, and I was shocked. The label on the jar said as big as day, 'Not To Be Taken Internally' – Poison!"

After that, Zeola said that she and Robin called the Boston Poison Control, and Robin asked them what would happen if somebody had taken alum over a period of time, and they told her that it would eventually close up their pipes or their lungs could collapse and they could die. He explained that alum tightens and pulls, so I called Dick Gregory and told him that we needed him. I told him that Marvin had been taking alum and Dick Gregory was upset.

"Dick Gregory told both Marvin and me that if I had not been giving Marvin all of those vitamins and that health drink, he wouldn't be here. Marvin asked us why she would do something like that. And I couldn't answer it because I felt so stupid because I didn't really check it out before giving it to him. But since it was coming from her, Marvin never questioned it or said for me not to give it to him."

Zeola said after that Marvin and Jan had a big fight and then he sent her home. She said that Dick Gregory put Marvin in some sort of bath water containing salt and vinegar to draw all of that poison out his system, and then Marvin contacted F. Lee Bailey and was going to press charges against Jan, but F. Lee Bailey advised Marvin that if he did that Zeola would be charged as an accomplice because she was the one giving it to Marvin, not Jan. So, in order to prevent Zeola from getting in trouble Zeola said that Marvin decided not to do it.

"Marvin never forgot that, and neither did I."

Zeola said that when Jan came to the house for the video tape and asked Zeola why she disliked her, Zeola said that she reminded Jan about the alum, and Jan denied ever providing it for Marvin.

"I couldn't believe that she sat right there on my sofa and denied it. She told me that she didn't do it."

During the time that Zeola was telling me about Jan a television show called THE MOTHER LOVE SHOW was being aired. The guests on the show were people who had hurt other individuals at some point in their lives, and they were coming to Mother Love, the host, hoping to seek forgiveness from the other person. They would tell their story to Mother Love and to the audience while the victim is offstage listening. Sight unseen, they would ask the victim for forgiveness. At the end of their plea, Mother Love would have the guest walk to the closed door and open it. If the victim was willing to forgive the guest, he/she would be standing in the opened doorway when the guest opened the door, and would generally hug the guest and tell them that they were forgiven. But if that victim did not forgive the guest, the opened doorway would be empty.

Zeola remembered the show and expressed her feelings about Jan to me by saying that if she were on THE MOTHER LOVE SHOW she would not come out of that door for Jan. Zeola said that Jan took, but she never gave.

That was a pretty strong statement I thought. So I asked Zeola what did she think made Jan this way, and she said, *"Her mother, Barbara."*

Zeola said that Jan's mother was dating a recording artist named Ed Townsend during the time that Marvin was at the studio recording LETS GET IT ON. Zeola said that Jan was supposedly at home crying because she had just broken up with her boyfriend so someone suggested to her mother to bring Jan down to the studio to watch Marvin record. *"Marvin said that she was adorable. He said that he fell in love with her almost immediately."*

Zeola said that she had to hand it to Jan in that she was very pretty. She said Jan's mother was white, so the mixed blood worked for Jan. Zeola called it 'that mixed looked.' *"She had the whole package. She had pretty hair, a beautiful complexion and a nice body.*

"I don't believe it was love at first sight for Jan. I don't believe that Jan even knew who Marvin was before she was introduced to him that day. It seemed to be her mother, Barbara, who made her pursue the relationship. Barbara was probably seeing dollar signs."

In the meantime, Zeola said that Marvin fell in love with Jan. *"He really loved her, even though she was a teenager. I'm sure that she hadn't even finished high school when they married."*

Maybe Jan had not completed high school when they got married but I am positive that she was older than sixteen. Marvin was still married to Anna when he met Jan, and Jan gave birth to two children during Marvin's marriage to Anna.

Even Zeola has admitted that she sometimes gets confused on the dates and time of events, but she still contends that Jan's relationship with Marvin was all about the money.

I think that Zeola truly believes that Jan's mother, Barbara, brought her teenage daughter to the studio that day for the possibility of marrying this great superstar who was at least seventeen years older than her daughter, for the sake of the almighty dollar. And I can truly understand her point because thus far my interviews with Zeola have mainly been about her father's ego and Marvin's money. Never have there been mention of family commitments or principals; just money and power.

Maybe this Barbara person was just trying to get her daughter discovered. Supposedly Jan has a great singing voice and wanted to become a professional singer. Jan's father supposedly was one of the great singers and song writers of the late 40's. So Jan must have been somewhat familiar with the music business. Therefore, she may very well had heard of Marvin. Regardless of the reason, Marvin obviously became love-struck almost immediately, and the rest is history.

"Marvin said that he really did love her, but I told him that he taught her a lot of things that wasn't good for her being so young. I told Marvin that he really created a monster. I told him that he was the older one, and that she followed his teachings. It started out that she was trying to please Marvin. But by the time she was twenty

137

one, she started coming out of that cocoon. It was as if she suddenly blossomed into womanhood."

Zeola said that she tried to explain to Marvin how girls change when they start to blossom. *"Girls want to be out there. I understand why Jan was doing what she was doing, but I didn't like the way she was doing it. She was so disrespectful to Marvin. She cheated on him all the time with most of his peers, even while she was in his house, and I didn't understand how her mother would sanction her behavior. My mother would have never put me out there to a man about seventeen years older than me just for the sake of money."*

Zeola believes that Marvin molded Jan to be the way she was. *"Jan probably wouldn't have fucked nearly as many of Marvin's friends if Marvin hadn't molded her into a cold-blooded freak."*

Zeola said what bothered her most was the fact that Jan's mother seemed to sanction the whole marriage thing even though Jan was still a child. She reiterated that she is sure it was all about the money.

"There was a time when I took Jan's side while we were on the road in Europe. I knew that Jan was seeing the guitar player because I was seeing the drummer and we all went to the movies together. They were sitting right next to me and they were holding hands, and he had his arms around her, but I wasn't paying much attention to what was going on because I was really into this drummer. I was so busy sneaking off because Marvin had already said that he didn't want me to have a relationship with anybody there. So Jan asked me if she could trust me. She really liked this guy. And I sort of understood at the time because even though Marvin was my brother, Jan was so young and this boy was her age. They must have been around nineteen or twenty, and she had already had two kids. So I could see a little bit of why she wanted to do this. I was really in her

corner. She had started getting loaded and just wanted to experiment, I guess. So I told her that I would never tell. But Marvin was always so smart. And he would always watch how she would watch different people. And he had a feeling that she liked this particular guitar player."

Zeola said that when they all came back from the movies, Jan asked her to cover for her. *"She told me that she was going to tell Marvin that she was coming down to my room, but she was going to this guitar player's room. So, Marvin came down to my room and of course she wasn't there. So he went straight to the boy's room. And that's where she was, and they were in the bed. They were really scared."*

Finally Marvin started kicking the door down and Zeola said that he hit the boy in the nose and wanted to fire him of course. She said that he told Jan that she could take her ass back to LA with the boy.

"That was very embarrassing for Marvin because the whole band knew that this had happened. And Marvin really needed a guitar player so he had to keep the boy until the end of the tour."

Zeola said that that was when Marvin recorded LIVE AT THE LONDON PALLADIUM. She said that on the back of the album Marvin put everybody's names with little sayings about things that they had said or done. Next to her name she said that he put "I'll never tell Gaye."

"Marvin got really mad at me because I didn't tell him about Jan. He made it very clear to me that he was my brother, and that I shouldn't let anything or anybody come between that. He said that our loyalty to each other is first and foremost. And he was right. I should have told him. I went back to my room and I was miserable because Marvin was mad at me for not telling, and he was about to send me home. In addition to that, Jan thought that I had told

139

Marvin. So I was just miserable because I had gotten into trouble over somebody who I didn't even particularly like."

Zeola was on a roll. She didn't smoke a joint or drink her wine or eat anything, and I was perfectly willing to continue recording her every word.

"I remember the last time Marvin saw his daughter, Nona. Her nickname was Pie, and we were at my little nephew's birthday party. Marvin had begged Jan to please allow Pie to come. Well, Jan said that she could come, but for only fifteen minutes. When Jan brought Pie to the big house, Marvin just hugged her and told her how much he loved her and told her how pretty she was."

Zeola said that Marvin and Jan's divorce had really turned ugly at that time. She said that they would have the most intense arguments that she had ever witnessed.

"My father's fights were tame compared to Marvin's because my father never used profanity. Because of the intense profanity, Marvin and Jan's arguments were almost frightening. I had never seen anything like it."

When Jan came to get Nona, Zeola said that her kids said that Nona ran and hid because she wanted to stay with Marvin because she hadn't seen him in a long time. But Jan dragged her out of the house, and Marvin never saw her again after that.

She said that she remembered one time when Jan had placed a restraining order out on Marvin. *"Jan and her mother lived in Hermosa Beach where very few blacks lived; especially, back in the 80's."*

Zeola said that Marvin went out there one night to talk to Jan and to see if he could see the kids. *"I was told that they went out on the beach to talk and things got loud so somebody called the police. And when the police showed up they beat Marvin up."*

140

Zeola said that they hit him so hard in one of his eyes that he almost went blind.

"I still believe that they would have stopped if Jan had asked them to, but Marvin said that she didn't and that bothers me to this day. It wasn't as if Marvin tried to break into her house or something. She invited him in."

Zeola said that she really did not want Marvin to go to Jan's house that night because the two of them had just had a big argument on the telephone, and this was one of those times Marvin broke the telephone by banging it down on the table.

"He just wanted to see his kids."

Looking at Zeola's face, I could tell that she must have been waiting a long time to express these feelings. She never picked up a joint during this entire session, nor did she accept a second glass of wine. She just sat on the sofa in basically one spot and continued to talk, and I continued to listen.

"After that Marvin found out that Jan and her mother had taken out a million dollar insurance policy on Marvin, so then he really thought that they were trying to kill him."

So now that they had both aired their feelings, Zeola said that they decided to do the project that Jan had requested. Later Zeola said that she found out that Jan was one of the executive producers on the show, and that was why she had so much input. *"Jan probably said that if she's gotta kiss ass to get me, and if it is more money for her, then she'll just have to kiss my ass."*

Jan arrived along with the camera crew for Zeola's interview, and it went the same as usual, Zeola said.

"Somebody would always ask me about how Marvin died. People are always asking why and how he died. Why can't they dwell on what he left us — his music? I answered them, but I saved most

141

things for my book, but I made sure to say positive things about the children."

It wasn't a surprise to me that Zeola made positive statements about Marvin's children because she always spoke well of them. Her only complaint to me was that she didn't see them often enough. She said that the few times that they were all together were good times.

Zeola said that when they went to the premiere of Jan's show in New York, she took her daughter, Nikki and her husband, Gary. She said that Jan took her daughter, Nona. When they got on the flight she said that everything was cool.

"At this time I was really being for real. I was thinking that we really were going to let bygones be bygones. I had gotten out how I felt and why I felt that way so I thought everything was okay. All of a sudden, at the event, things were back like it was when we were on the road. People were bringing other people up to me and introducing me as Marvin's sister instead of going to Jan, and she didn't seem to like it."

Zeola reminded me that Jan was not Marvin's wife when he died. She said that most articles were calling Jan the widow, but Jan wasn't his widow. They were divorced. *"Jan divorced him!"* Zeola said as she raised her voice to an excitable level.

"What bothers me now is when I read articles where Jan calls herself Marvin's widow. The Widow Gaye. She is not his widow." Zeola exclaimed. *"They were divorced long before Marvin died. She had no status with him when he died other than being the mother of his children."*

Zeola claimed that Jan's attitude was partially why Nona had not become a super star yet.

"If it had not been for Jan's attitude, and the improper training and up-bringing, Nona would have probably done better by now." Zeola said.

Nona seems to be a beautiful and talented actress, and she seems to have done pretty good by Hollywood's standards so I wasn't quite sure what Zeola meant by that statement. I don't think that she meant any harm against Nona. Her anger still seemed to be directed towards Jan.

When I asked Zeola her opinion as to why Marvin continued to pursue Jan, even after he thought that she had tried to poison him, she surprised me with her answer.

"There are certain herbs and roots that you can buy and put in people's food to make them do what you want them to do. And I think that in addition to the alum, something else was being given to Marvin without our knowledge. Maybe it was put in the weed or something, I don't know. There's stuff out there that make people stay with you, there's stuff that can make you love them and put up with anything that you do and there's even stuff that can make you bring your money home. There are all kinds of herbs out there that people use."

I've heard of people in the Deep South using 'roots' for other methods of getting what they want, but for some reason I have never taken it seriously. That sounds strange coming from someone whose spiritual encounters are very real. I suppose there are those out there who probably think the same thing about me and my experiences. So I shut my mouth and continued to listen to her.

"Well, Marvin was going through all of these crazy things, and he couldn't understand why he was going through all this. And he couldn't explain why he kept feeling for her the way that he was. He just couldn't stop going after her. Yet, when they were together all they did was argue, fuss and fight. He could run down to us all the

143

things that she had done to him. He named all the friends that he knew that she had fucked. He talked about how he had caught her. He talked about how she didn't believe in God; she threatened him with the kids yet he still wanted to be with this girl. She could make a phone call to him, and he would go right to her. And it never lasted long. That's what herb and roots do. It doesn't make you happy, but it will do whatever needs to be done at the time." Zeola said that Marvin thought that Jan was putting something in his food.

When Dick Gregory heard all of this he said, *"You know what, man? It sounds like something is on you because Black men just don't do stuff like this."* Zeola explained that Dick Gregory was talking about the way Marvin kept chasing after Jan.

Zeola said that Dick Gregory suggested sending for someone whom he knew might be able to help. *"She could tell you if anything was wrong with Marvin,"* He said.

"I will never forget her. Her name was Mother Gibson. Anyway, Marvin sent for her because he thought that Jan was putting something in his food, and she came out to California."

Zeola's husband, Gary, was scared of anything that dealt with witchcraft. Zeola said that he would say, *"Oh no, they're dealing with the spirits! I don't want anything to do with that."* But he ended up bringing the lady to Marvin anyway.

"And when she and her daughter got out of the car, Gary said that they left a terrible smell in the car. We later found out that the smell was from the oils that she used to ward off evil. And she gave it to Marvin to put on, and he wore it faithfully. She also went through the house. I don't remember where Jan was at the time. I think she was in San Francisco visiting her half sister. Anyway, Mother Gibson went through the house and found snakes in the house. Yes, real snakes. And she informed us that these were the worst kind of snakes. She said that these were the types of snakes that were used to do harm to others. She asked Marvin where he got his cocaine from,

144

and he named a few people. But he also said that he would sometimes get it from Jan."

The woman told Marvin, *"Honey, you know what? You've been smoking bat wing!"* And then Zeola said that the woman advised Marvin not to ever take anything from Jan again. She said that that's what was keeping him with her. *"That was when Marvin moved back with our mother and father and left Jan to live alone in their home in Hidden Hills."*

Zeola said that Marvin continued his relationship with Mother Gibson and did finally get better.

This portion of Zeola's story confused me a bit because in the end when the government took everything from Marvin, Zeola said that Jan was not living in the house in Hidden Hills. She said that only Marvin was there. And unfortunately I am not at liberty to ask Zeola to clarity this portion of her story, but going by the amount of times Marvin and Jan seemed to have fought and then got back together, and then fought again, I guess somewhere along the line, Marvin ended up at the Hidden Hills house, and Jan must have moved on to another location.

This couple truly seemed to have been on an unbelievable rollercoaster of drama. No wonder Marvin wanted some peace in his life.

I don't know what type of relationship Jan and Zeola have today; especially since, according to Zeola, Jan has paid her not to tell her story, and I really don't much care because these people seem to beat to a drum that I'm not at all familiar with.

CHAPTER
12

HAWAII

Marvin left Jan and went to Hawaii when she started dating Rick James, according to Zeola. She said that that really killed Marvin inside. Things were never right between the couple after that. Zeola compared them with oil and water. *"They tried to blend, but they just couldn't. Marvin would throw up to Jan all the things that she had done that he didn't like, and the fights would start all over again."*

While Marvin was staying in Hawaii Zeola said that Jan had dropped their son off to stay with Alberta in Los Angeles. During that time the baby got sick so Alberta called Marvin in Hawaii. According to Zeola, Jan told the media that she had gone to Hawaii and left the baby there with Marvin, but Zeola said that that was not true.

Zeola said that Marvin had called his mother that Friday and was told that Jan had left their son with her. The next day she said that Marvin called again and her mom told Marvin that the baby was sick with a high fever. By Sunday Zeola said that Marvin had become very concerned because Alberta still had not heard from Jan.

"Marvin really loved Bubbie. Well, of course he loved Nona, whom he nicknamed, 'Pie' too, but now he had a natural son. So Bub was his heart and Pie was his love. He would say that she was his bouncy little girl. And Bub was the man."

On Monday Marvin called Zeola and said, *"Zee, hop on a plane and bring Bubbie to me."* So Zeola's friend Robin took her to the airport with the baby. Zeola said that she stayed with Marvin and the baby for a few days and then returned home.

When Jan finally surfaced and realized that Zeola had taken the baby to Marvin, Zeola said that she called the police and accused Zeola of kidnapping the baby. Marvin kept Bubbie for more than a month. During that time Zeola said that Jan had tried to get her arrested for kidnapping, but it did not happen. Jan said that the environment in Hawaii was not suitable for the baby, but Zeola disagreed.

"Marvin had very nice accommodations for his kid at that time." Zeola said. She also said that after she left Hawaii, Marvin took care of the baby himself with no outside help.

When Zeola told me about this incident it only confirmed my thoughts of Marvin's good spirit and unconditional love. Let's face it the average man wouldn't have given a second thought to leaving that kid with his grandmother. The average Super Star would have never looked back. Although surrounded by drug demons and a highly dysfunctional family, facing issues that most of us can't even begin to relate to, Marvin called for his sick child, and literally nursed him back to health by himself.

While Marvin was in Hawaii Zeola said that he wrote a letter to Jan's mother, Barbara. She said that he blamed Barbara for a lot of what had occurred between him and Jan.

"He felt that Barbara was the force behind everything that Jan had done."

Zeola said that Marvin gave the letter to Frankie to give to Barbara, but somehow Alberta got hold of it, and Barbara never received it.

"When Marvin came home my mom gave the letter back to Marvin. She always liked to keep peace, so she probably wouldn't let Frankie give it to Barbara because she probably thought it was too harsh. But then Marvin gave it to me. I don't know why he gave it to me, but I've held on to it until now."

Zeola said that Barbara passed away a few years ago, and Jan never saw the letter. Shortly after Zeola called me to tell me that Jan had paid her off not to finish the book, she called again to request the letter because she said that Jan wanted to burn the letter up. That was to be the final cover-up, I guess, but I felt so strongly that Marvin wanted his story told, and the letter was a part of his story. I do not believe that I would have ever been given that letter if it were not meant for me to see. All the signs that I have received thus far seem to have been telling me that it is time to redeem Marvin's spirit. So I didn't give it to Zeola for Jan to burn.

When Zeola called and requested the letter I asked her why she would hold on to something that she felt so strongly about all these years and then just suddenly burn it up for the sake of a few dollars. She had no answer other than she needed the money. When I reminded her that I had already advised her of the possibility of a sell-out, she had no comment other than the immediate need for money.

What I found most interesting during our conversation was that Zeola did not seem bothered by the fact that I was not going to allow the letter to be burned. Not once did she ask me to please give it to her, or tell me just how much it meant to her to have it destroyed. Instead, she seemed very matter-of-fact about it. She just gave me the information, and accepted my answer with no other comments other than it was Jan's request.

I had been working with Zeola for a long time, and I got to know her pretty well, and deep down inside I believe that she still wants her story to be told, as well as this letter to be exposed. She took the money, I believe, because she needed it, and was very accustomed to selling off anything of Marvin's for the sake of a dollar instead settling down to a good ole nine to five job like most of us. But I suppose that it must be very difficult for someone to go from having everything in life handed to you on a silver platter to having nothing except a few memories and some old memorabilia.

Zeola might not be very happy with my beliefs that Marvin did not get the help he needed from the people closest to him, but I am pretty sure that she will not resent me for completing this book. It will only give her more of the attention that she seems to desperately crave. Last I heard she was starring in a play down South about Marvin's life. I was told that she and the producer figured if they put the shows on in small towns in the South that the owners of Marvin's music in Hollywood would never find out. But I guess that did not work out. Maybe she was paid to stop what she was doing again.

Joe Burns, a Baltimore Sun reporter wrote: *The play is scheduled to run in Baltimore amid controversy, however, Zoela Gaye, Marvin's sister, who once starred as herself in the production, has pulled out. Friday she said the playwright has been threatened with an injunction and a lawsuit if the play continues to run.*

Also, I have been informed that she is attempting to produce something in Detroit Michigan and then throughout the country. I wish her luck. Reliving the glitz and glamour of Hollywood seems to be very important to Zeola.

When I read the letter that Marvin had written to Jan's mother, Barbara, from Hawaii my heart went out to him because the pain and confusion that he was experiencing was so evident. At the same time I could see why Alberta did not give the letter to her. Zeola has said many times how much her mother believed in the sanctity of marriage and this letter obviously would not have helped restore the young couple's troubled marriage.

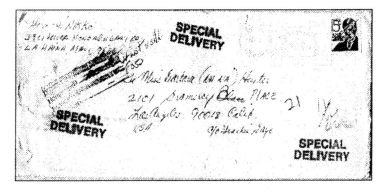

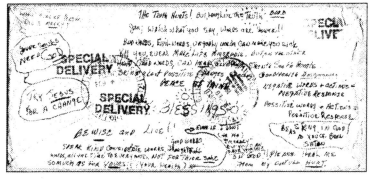

Audrey King Lewis

The First of a series of Letters.
Copys too go too.
B. Stroum
E. Townsend
+ To be inserted in auto biography.

Jan 31, 80"
"Maui"
12:37

To The Grandmother of my Precious One"

1. In your heart you knew you're a hypocrite, You love One more than Buffy, And if you say you don't you're a Lyer too.

2. You would be lying if you said you wanted My mother to spend Equal time with the One And that it would please you if One loved her as much as you.

3. I Know your motives, I know how you are deep inside, and you hate me for my insight. I know more about you than you imagine. ["Mrs Barbara Hunter"?]

   I think you are a perfect illustration of a sick, white, Pig society. Your cold and ruthless satan inspired Philosophies and lifestyles, are an abomination to my sweet and innocent and highly impressionable, little girl. You have already Fucked up one beautifull Godsoul, you which you should be repentive and hardworking in every rightfull way, to heal. Yes to heal the nearly irre-parable scars your ungodly soul and irresponsible cmotherhood has cut, deep into her being.

   What have I done? The Father of the child you love so dear. One Half the source of her brilliance is mine (maybe more) One half of her Genious + Personality is mine (maybe more) One Half the lugs around your produced cold white neck are mine, One Half the eyes you think are so

152

Cont.　　　　　　　(2)

pretty, One kept the soft, sweet, warm body that you managed to help divide from me. seriously, when you recomended your mindless daughter to press charges against me. There bye doing irreparable damage to me as an artist and to my professional career. A career already tedering on the brink of desaster. A career that should be sheltered o protected at least for the childrens sake (Insurance, College, money, clothes food etc) I am their father

And Jan, she says she loves me, but no women who loves a man would do the kind of things she's done And what had I done to deserve the Jet magazine and other major newspublications Printings: Marvin Gaye arrested by hermosa beach police for assult and battary On Jan Gaye: People will stop buying my records on these kind of lies, And on the other hand we all knew you were both busy helping to build Teddy Pender graces career. Did I assult and battary Jan? Why did you really recommend the press charges? It was revenge wasn't it! Pure and simple cold blooded revenge. For what? Takeing my children from you wicked home? looking at you with accusing eyes? Maybe because you think I hate you cause youre white. I hate you cause youre sick! and proud of it. Just like your daughter whom you have personally misguided. And now you have my one in your so called capable care.

You Probably hate Mother too, Cause she is very capable, And Probably reminds you of all the women youre not. But should have been. She Will know the truth!! But wait! Now you see yourself trying to make up for the useless, wasted years of endless Pleasure

153

Cont.   ③

and sinfull delights. Recomended of coarse to your weak daughter (whom you are really jealous of) who cannot see the destructive path she's taking trying to emulate your strange and empty existance.

Hence, the deep guilt trip you harbor hence your attempt to atone for your selfish wickedness, hence your inept attempt to love nurchure and raise the womenchild of your unbemothered daughter. Of course you have no training (And no qualification for and most of all, you are unworthy to tamper with the life of a child like me.

What will you teach her? Your ungodly retoric? How to smoke, How to cry good? How to be nuirotic? How to be white? How to smoke? Smart Cake? Cuss? (your friends) Will you teach her that its alright to kiss a filthy dog in the mouth (you think dogs are just as good as people and just as clean too, don't you?) Lick her ice cream cone like your dog does yours? Will you have her pattern her sex life after yours (Proud!) What about Cuss? Her spiritual life after yours? (what's that?) Or perhaps teach her your learned white intellect (what a smart little pretty girl.) But who will teach her WISDOM!! Was it you, that recomended Jan take three shots to dry up her milk after having Que? Are you Wise Barbara? Who will teach her respect for womanhood & motherhood and naturalness, you Granny? Do you have respect for God and his Creation? No You already told me how you feel about God!

Cont. ④

Who well teach her to have empathy and compassion
in her heart? That, you dont watch a man take
a brutal and unjust beating, for basically
trying to save a marriage by trying to communicate
with an unreasonable, disrespectfull, beligerent
young sickie, who, after all the shit! shes digged me
into would not give me the courtesy of a res
pectfull half hour audience, wellout trying
to prove shee as superior as Q the Q
am the man! When she knew shee not, she knew
shee ill. she knows shee bad she knows she wrong.
ask L.A. after a while I decided I would be
heard and proceeded to engage her, and hold
her down (in the sand) untill she decides to
listen to me for the last time. Com Life, My Life
(the children life) at whiteh point she decides she would.
and, like her undecisive self she reconsiders and
decides she wont. frustrated! I become angry and
say, if you dont listen to me am going to take the
children again! at which point she goes screaming
down the beach for the police (white style) the
self respecting black women would call the
white satanic merciless pigs (Hermosa Beach
all white cops) on the father of her children, especially
when there are other ways to work it out. Im not
unreasonable, and my love for you is strong
enough, that a few sweet words of kindness and
repentance would certainly have been enough
to bring me around as far as the kids were con
cerned. It was unnesesary and stupid, and she knew
it. and you do to. But you alls pride and inborn
white hatred blood, and cold heartless consideration

Cont 3.

(all from Satan, who wants to destroy me)
would have you put me in a position
where where I could possibly HAVE lost my life. She &
Bubby Fatherless? You may even like that Idea
physiologically; I mean why should they
have a decent loving Father, She never had
one (Ha Ha) She says She loves me, yet after
coming to my defense somewhat, after seeing
the results of her actions (again, As Tho she
enjoys tempting the laws of Fate) Her ration-
al, Unthinking Passiveness to her fleery and FREEZY
uncontrollable Emotionalism submitting submitting without shame to the first neurotic
suggestion (a white womens trait) that her con
fussed and impure blood and body mind
and brain dictate without regard to consequence

A kind of strange Power trait, womanly
a womenlly satisfaction a Power to weild
over the defenceless man (Emotional warfare)
Tears, Super Emotionalism Fake sickness, acting
physically weak, neurotic states mind (Continues)
useing the children etc. What Marvelous
weapons to use against me. And all because
I proved to you that I really love you, Gave
you the Power!! I gave you the Power, me the fool.

Its like a Movie, a like movie. Its like
saying something bad is suppose to happen if I do this
thing. I wonder if it will (a womens natural curiosity)
I wonder what will happen, I cant wait to see what I
create. What Power! I can create some thing good and
Possitive (no fun) with this Power. Or, I can create some

-cont.

(6)

deep serious shit. What Power! (smart huh Barbara) yes! I know you. I'm not only smart, I'm choosen as you will probably live to see. Blessed, loved, and respected (before meeting you and Jan) I am Superior to you, and Magnificent. And now that I've had a chance to cool out a little best of all I am undaunted.* By now I dont ever expect to get any real respect, repentance or understanding from you. And I'm writing you this letter cause I hold you responsible for it. all. All blood is on your hands!! You will be punished.

Anyway after watching hearing about your pig cop friends beating me and my subsequent arrest. Was there any empathy for me? From you? Did you ask if I were injured seriously? Did you wonder how I felt? Was it a good feeling to know that the police had beat me unmercifully? Do you care that Jees Father has a demented black eye? Do you care that my retina is injured? You think I got what I deserve dont you? The Movie! You girls love it. It would be great for the movie (life) if I lose one eye, huh. See what you've created Jan + Barb. Yes sir Jumping Movie, Jan is the producer & Barbara you're the director.

More: after spending a couple of hours In the cell. I was told I could not be released unless I had 6 hundred dollar cash, cause you were has just pressed charges. After breaking

Cont   ⑦

(my heart by fucking old bad feet (Funky)
(she likes Funk) kratty dick himself. She Presser
Charges, After exposing all my assets in
the Paper (there by taking food and lodging from
the children in the future and herself, all
to your delight grow jealous Remember!
stripping me of my last few hidden treasures
and Publicly filing for divorce (when it could
have been done Quitely for the childrens sake and
because I really didnt deserve it (Careen)
She pressed charges! After seeing me bleeding
and enjured and seriously hurt more than
you know (never really enqured as to my state
of health afterwards) She Pressed charges" On
MARVIN GAYE SUPER STAR, who deserves NO CONSIDER
ATIon For NoThinG GoOD HesDONE. nothing worth
Protecting, Nothin' about me deserving in your
eyesight. Lets fuck him good while hes down
the WHite WoMeNS WAy. PRESS CHARGES Against
THAT NIGGER!! What ever you rationall &
justifications you all have done me a terrible
injustice & Wronging did you all take your power
to far? Use it to strongly? Were you frightened
then weak. Are you repentive NO!

I can just hear you Bartona, Press
Charges It will go well for you in havarce
court. It will cool him off. Cost him money
(more money) hes too strong, we need to break him.
If I had some strong white blood in me,
I would have shot all three of you. You Jean, and
officer Collins. Then myself. You know how you all
are. But my Blackness (Gods chosen) close to

Cont.   (8)

earth God and sanity would never allow me to pull off such a stupid action, altho I had plenty of reason..

Well Jen, as per usual I have some good advice for you that you will probably shit on. And I know that there is no chance for future reconciliation Cause you will hate me now, that you know I Hate your Mother. My advice:

Youre Mothers Voice is the Voice of Satan. Words are Power! Consider her words carefully before you act. And, may God have mercy on the Fee.

Feb. 1st
3:55
Mom

I Love God

do you all?
BYBBWill   Will oie......

"I really wish that Nona had been given the chance to know her father because he loved her very much. I would love to have her and Bubbie visit my family. I wish that they were able to be around my daughters, Kim and Nikki, so that they could hear the good things about their father. They never got to know how much he loved them."

Shortly after Zeola returned to Los Angeles from Hawaii a well-known British promoter, Jessie Krueger set up a London tour for Marvin.

"Marvin invited my mom and my aunt Tolie and me to come along on the tour because he needed someone to take care of Bubbie. My mom's friend Jewel came along too. We all flew over together."

Zeola said that she appreciated England, but the tour didn't go so well. Marvin didn't have all of his people with him over there to organize everything. Plus, she said that Jan came over there and brought her half sister who was designing a lot of Marvin's suits. She said that Marvin and Jan seemed to have made some sort of peace during that time, but Marvin told Zeola that he still felt that Jan had something up her sleeve.

"Marvin told me that he didn't trust Jan so he asked me to keep an eye on them, but they all stayed together in Marvin's room a lot so that was kind of difficult for me. Jan and her sister didn't include me in very much, so I spent a lot of time with my mom and Aunt Tolie and Jewel."

CHAPTER
13

ADDICTION

"Marvin was despondent about everything. He was still concerned about the fact that Jan had tried to poison him, he was getting death threats while on his London tour, and the promoters weren't giving him his money."

Zeola said that Marvin would either stay at the big house with their mother or at her house. She said that he didn't want to go anyplace else, and he felt he couldn't be creative.

"Both Marvin and Jan were on crack cocaine," Zeola stated with all sincerity. She said that sometimes Jan would call Marvin over to her house so that he would bring cocaine to her and her friends."

"One night while Marvin and I were watching a football game on television and Jan called to get Marvin to bring cocaine to her and her friends. I didn't want to give the phone to Marvin because I didn't want him to go over there. I thought that that was a waste of cocaine. Marvin kept the powered cocaine and I knew that they would have to cook it up. I felt that that was such a waste."

At first I did not understand what Zeola meant by 'cooking it up' but later found out that it meant the separation of pure cocaine from the added powdery substance used to stretch the cocaine. In the 70's it was generally known as 'free basing.' Evidently, powdered cocaine is placed in a small container that sits in boiling water, and the powdered cocaine is then sprinkled with baking soda and water. The heat from the boiling water will cause the powdered cocaine to separate causing the pure cocaine to turn into somewhat of a gooey substance, which when cooled; it hardens and becomes pure rock cocaine. The 'cut', dissipates into a liquid form which is discarded. The pipe that is generally used is usually made of something similar to Pyrex because it must withstand the heat of the boiling water. The rock is then placed on a screen of some sort in a glass pipe and the lower portion of the pipe is generally filled with a rum or water. Heat administered to the bottom of the pipe causes the rock to melt. The smoke from the melting rock cocaine is then inhaled. When I asked what was the purpose for putting the Rum or water in the bottom of the pipe, I was told that it takes away some of the harshness of the smoke. However, addicts do sometimes cook it up without a liquid in the bottom of the pipe. I suppose that is the user's choice.

My other curiosity was about the darkness around the nostrils. I have seen several celebrities who, without makeup, have had that almost black look surrounding the nostrils, and I often wondered what caused it. I was told that it was a result of sucking up hot air when there was no cocaine left on the screen of the pipe. The heat from the pipe literally burns the skin as the overly anxious user continues to inhale hot air in hopes of locating some remaining residue. I was told that the purpose of the rock versus the powder is that it gives a quicker and stronger rush than the powder. But the downside of it is that crack is much more addictive than powder for some reason.

After understanding the process for making the rock, I still did not understand why modern crack cocaine is sold at a cheaper price than powdered cocaine. I was also told that crack cocaine today is cheaper because someone came up with the brilliant idea to sell rocks already prepared, thus adding all sorts of addictive chemicals to it, so that by the time the buyer gets it it is filled with so much junk that it can be sold for much less money. The seller still makes more money because it attracts a larger population, especially the minority communities because it is more affordable. This is known as a designer drug. It is no longer pure, but mixed with even more addictive chemicals than the powdered cocaine. I guess that is why even today, some people still cook their own or will make sure to be present while it is being cooked up. I was informed that in the 70's and early 80's designer drugs had not yet been created, so I suppose that Marvin and his friends had no choice but to 'cook up' their own.

The few times that I was graced with Marvin's presence I don't remember ever seeing any signs of disfigurement around his nose, so I do believe that Zeola was telling the truth when she said that Marvin did not delve heavily into crack cocaine. However, I will admit that I didn't have the sense to look for anything like that on people back in those days. It is only of recent times that I have been privy to seeing anyone with the discoloration.

Zeola said that since she wasn't doing crack, Marvin gave it to her to hold because he didn't like doing it and wanted to stop. He said to her, *"Zee, no matter what I do or what I say, don't give it to me."* So she said that she agreed. Zeola said that he repeated, *"I don't care what I say. Don't do it. He said to only dish it out to him a little at a time. He would ask me to make a couple of cigarettes at a time, and that's what I did."*

But Zeola said that one day Jan called and she heard Marvin say, *"Okay."* And Zeola said that she knew what that meant.

"Jan was asking him to come over. She would use him like that because she knew how badly he wanted to be with her and to see his kids. So, he asked me for the coke, and I wouldn't give it to him. He said, 'Give me the coke!' and once again I said 'No because you told me not to give it to you no matter what you say.' He was getting upset with me, but I wouldn't do it."

Earlier Zeola said that Marvin had promised her $10,000. She said that she was to receive it that following Monday.

Marvin told her that if she didn't give him the cocaine that he would not give her the $10,000 that he had promised her. Well, she said that she started crying because that hurt her feelings so bad. So she said, *"Here, take your fucking cocaine."* And she gave it to him.

"He knew that I was upset because he knew that I didn't want him to smoke the rock. I just had a thing about it. I just didn't want him to do it. So, I continued to cry, and he took the coke and went over to Jan's house. When Marvin came home the next day he told me that he and Jan had made a pact that they weren't going to do crack anymore. He said that he had talked her into breaking up all the paraphernalia and throwing it away, and they flushed the cocaine down the toilet. He said that he didn't like the wild changes he would go through with the rock."

Zeola said that men don't handle that part of cocaine very well. She said that's why Marvin used to say that they call it 'the girl or the lady.' It always had a woman's name because women handled cocaine better than men. She suggested that men generally do crack cocaine because they want to have sex. *"It's not just to get high. It's more of a sexual thing with men."* Zeola's opinion of women is that they do it generally to kick back. She suggested that they usually don't want to have sex, but if they are offered more crack then they will give it up. She said that is why women who are hooked on crack are called strawberries because that's what they will do. She said that they give up sex for drugs.

There is something about the word 'strawberries' that still continues to confuse me because I don't see the connection between the word 'strawberries' and sex. It is probably just a nickname that was given to hookers on crack.

I've asked several female users about their opinion on how crack cocaine affects them, and their answers were a bit different than Zeola's. They said that the use of crack cocaine often times heighten their desire for sex. However, I did not speak to any 'strawberries.' A couple of men said that they enjoy just kicking back after the use of crack cocaine. They confirmed the fact that when one is laid back one might enjoy the notion, but the actual act of having sex is not an absolute necessity. So I guess the saying, 'different strokes for different folks' apply in this case too.

I kept in mind that Zeola had stated to me several times before this particular session that she did not always have orgasms while having sex, so this just might be an example of why she thinks the way she does about the sexual affects that crack might have on a person.

"The men don't care whether you want to do it or not, they're aroused so they just want sex. Most of the time they only want some head anyway because that's basically what crack is about for them. Most users' dicks flop anyway because it's sometimes difficult to get hard. So, mostly they just want their dicks sucked."

Sometimes Zeola's frankness was a little embarrassing, but I enjoyed listening to her. I think that her ability to tell a story has a bit of the same qualities that Marvin gave to his music. I am sure that she knows that she cannot speak for all crack users, but her point of view about crack cocaine has certainly given me a new awareness. I always wondered what the difference was between crack cocaine and powdered, and now I know. So I continued to listen without interruption.

"So when Marvin came back he said that he had thought about me all that night. He finally understood why I was crying. He understood that I just didn't want him doing crack. I knew a little bit about what the deal was, but I didn't know the depth of what crack cocaine was about at that time. But I knew that Jan was just

using him to get what she wanted. She never called him unless she wanted something. And I hated seeing him fall into that trap."

The next day Jan called Marvin, and Zeola said that she heard him tell her that he wasn't coming back over there. According to Zeola they argued and argued because Marvin reminded her that they had made a pact not to do that anymore. Zeola said that apparently it wasn't over for Jan because she continued to argue.

"But Marvin didn't go. I said all of that to explain just how strong Marvin was. He quit doing crack cold turkey. And he didn't go back to it. It was always amazing to me how when he was determined to do something, he would just do it."

Zeola told me of a syndicate of drug dealers who handled all of the drugs in California. She would not mention their names, but said that Marvin got hooked up with these people because of the drugs. She said that they would just give it to him just because he was Marvin.

"Sometimes he would pay for it, but most of the time they would just give it to him."

Marvin told Zeola that he had figured out that Jan was hanging out with these men because of the drugs. "He told me that he had gotten proof that she was seeing one of the guys."

So, one day Marvin called Zeola into his room and said, *"Zee, take a look at this shit."* Zeola said that it was a baggy with about ten big rocks of cocaine in it.

"They were big like golf balls. I had never seen anything like that in my life. So I asked Marvin what it was because it did not look real. He said that the Black Promoters had sent it over. And then he said that he wasn't going to smoke that shit."

When you are hooked on crack, Zeola said that you just don't have crack next to you and you don't use it, but she said that Marvin did just that. She remembered Marvin saying that he felt that Jan was behind this guy sending him all those drugs. He told Zeola that he thought that it might have been poison in it because he couldn't figure out why they would send him this without him asking for it.

All that I could envision at that moment was Marvin besieged by demons.

"Later, one of my nephews smoked it and said that it was the baddest shit that they had ever had. Even then, Marvin never touched it. He still believed that Jan and the promoters wanted to kill him."

As time went by Zeola said that paranoia was taking over Marvin's life. She said that he went over to a drug dealer's house, and they decided to go over to the racetrack. Marvin told Zeola that he really didn't want to go but he went anyway. *"And that's when he decided to jump out of the car. He said that the men in the car were conspiring, and he could hear it in their voices. So he decided to jump."*

It doesn't appear that Marvin jumped out of that car to kill himself like the media suggested, but instead, he jumped to escape the demons in his mind.

Zeola said that Marvin was all scratched up when he called her house and asked Gary to come and pick him up and take him to his mom's house where she tended to his wounds and bruises with alcohol and peroxide.

"Gary came home and told me that Father kept coming into the room and asking Maw why she was putting all that stuff on Marvin and tending to him so much. He accused Maw of being too close to Marvin to be his mother. He told Maw that she and Marvin didn't act like mother and son. And Maw thought that that was so out of place that she didn't even respond. She just looked at Father in disgust. Marvin got really pissed and Maw calmed him down. But Father would come back again and again asking her why she was

still working on Marvin. Later, Marvin called Gary back to the house that night and asked him to bring him a pastrami sandwich from the Johnny's Pastrami. That was Marvin's favorite sandwich along with a pineapple crush soda. The place was open 24 hours, so Gary went by there and bought what Marvin had asked for, and then took it to Marvin at the big house. Before Gary left my house, I told him to tell Marvin that I love him, and I told Gary to give Marvin a big hug for me. As many times as Marvin has called for Gary I had never asked him to do anything like that before. And when Gary came home, I was very concerned if he had told Marvin what I said. And he said yeah. He told me that Marvin said, "Tell Zee that I love her very much too, and give her this hug back, but I ain't kissing you." So we laughed about that. It really made me feel good that Marvin had said that."

After Marvin's last tour, Zeola said that he would have bouts of rage, and nobody could talk with him but her. She said whenever Marvin was staying at the big house Alberta would call her and ask her to come to calm him down. She said that Marvin's emotions were sometimes out of control, and even though she loved her brother, she was trying to make a life for herself now that the tours were over, but she would still go and talk to Marvin every time her mother called.

"I was trying desperately to have a life. Finally, I told Marvin to just come home and stay with me. That saved me from running back and forth to the big house. He seemed comfortable there. The only problem was that we lived on Olympic Boulevard and it was a main street so people would want to come to the house just to see Marvin. I had to finally put a note on my door telling people that if they didn't bother to call, don't knock."

This was during the time of the Grammies, and Marvin was working on the national anthem.

169

Even though Marvin wasn't doing crack, Zeola admitted that he was still doing cocaine, and she said that she was worried about him because some of the things he would say and do seemed irrational. Zeola said that he would go around all day and not put any clothes on. He would just keep on his robe, his straw hat and slippers and sit around the house all day.

"A lot of times my mom would call me and ask me to come up to the big house to get Marvin because he would be arguing with Father. She wouldn't say what they were arguing about."

When you are doing cocaine like Marvin was, Zeola said that it can make your whole personality change. She said that Marvin had become sort of evil and mean.

"It wasn't like it was on the road when he did cocaine. His whole disposition had changed. The cocaine seemed like it had finally taken its toll on him. I don't know if it was because somebody was giving him something different in the cocaine, but his mind was starting to go. I don't know if he was getting the bat wings again or not. And if so, he couldn't be protected now because he wasn't taking his vitamins and B12 shots like he was on the road. He was just doing the coke and drinking heavily, and arguing with Jan on the telephone. So I would try to calm him down because he wouldn't listen to anybody but me."

According to Zeola, Marvin started getting worse. One day while he was at Zeola's house he said, *"Zee, do you hear that?"* Zeola said, *"Hear what?"* He told her that he could hear Jan and someone talking. Zeola once again refused to mention that person's name. I assumed that this was the same drug dealer that she didn't want to reveal earlier.

Zeola said that she asked Marvin what they were saying, and he got that look on his face like he was really listening to what they were saying. *"He said that it was coming through the telephone wires. He said that Jan was talking to this person right then. And then he picked up the phone and he would hear them talking and then ask me to listen. Of course I couldn't hear anything. And that's when he started going down."*

Whenever Marvin would go back to the big house, he would be in his room and tell Zeola that a man had Jan tied up to a chair and she was calling him. Zeola said that he would say that a man was doing all sorts of crazy sexual things to Jan, and she was crying out to Marvin. And then he would say, *"They know I'm listening, so they want to know what I think about it."*

Zeola said that Marvin couldn't understand why she couldn't hear it.

"He would constantly ask me if I thought he was losing his mind because he could hear her and I couldn't. And I told him that I believed that he could hear it, but I just could not. This goes back to what I had said about spirits and demons. I knew that I couldn't dispute the fact that Marvin could hear something because I truly believe that he could because I know that demons are strong, and you can hear them and see them if you are receptive of them; especially, if you're doing drugs. You can hear voices. And every once in a while he would go over to that man's house and Jan's car would be right where he said it would be."

Zeola said that Marvin wouldn't go inside the man's house and make trouble or anything. She said that he would just come back home satisfied that Jan was exactly where he said she would be. She said that Marvin went through this a lot because he was obsessed with Jan being with this man who had all these drugs. Zeola said that Marvin felt that the man was taking advantage of her. He would get very explicit when he would describe what the syndicate was doing with her.

"It got to a point where I had decided that it was over for anybody who came to that house to bring drugs to Marvin. It was time for me to start trying to get Marvin some help. Robin and I made a few calls and had found a place to take him. We had already made arrangements to take him to this place on Monday, and he was killed on that Sunday."

Zeola said that she had a hard time trying to convince Marvin to go there. "I told him that it was a private place where stars go to get rehabilitated, and nobody ever knew about it."

For the first time it sounded as if somebody in that family was trying to help Marvin, I thought. But it was just too late.

According to Zeola, a lot of people were angry with her during that time because she spent a lot of time up at the big house blocking the drug dealers. She said that Robin stayed with her a lot of times.

"What was interesting was that even though fewer drugs were coming in for Marvin, he could still hear the voices. He would insist that he could hear Jan. He would still pick up the telephone and insist that he could hear Jan's whole conversations with this man, who Zeola will not mention. Marvin was so unhappy. He talked a lot about wanting to die, and that's when he started telling me how he wanted the arrangements for his funeral. I told him that I didn't want to hear any of that, but he told me that I had to. He told me that he had taught me enough about life that he was sure that I could handle things for him. So I listened."

CHAPTER
14

HERE, MY DEAR

Zeola informed me at the beginning of the session that she wanted to talk about Marvin's conflicts with Berry Gordy and Motown Records, but because there have been so many articles and books written about the relationship between Marvin and Mr. Gordy I could not imagine anything else that needed to be said. Still, Zeola insisted that Marvin had shared personal experiences with her about the Gordy family that had yet to be published. The moment she mentioned 'personal experiences' with the Gordy family another flag went up for me because I had previously worked for Mr. Gordy for about two years, and not only did I learn to respect the man more than ever before, I know how much he likes his privacy. So writing something about him and his family did not set well with me, but Zeola was the story teller, not me, so I decided to simply record what she had to say and hoped that nothing would make Mr. Gordy's lawyers come down on our heads.

Once again I had prepared one of Zeola's favorite pasta dishes and wanted to quickly serve it up so that we could get started. I nuked the pasta that I had prepared that morning consisting of linguini, virgin olive oil, garlic and jumbo shrimp topped with freshly grated parmesan cheese and emptied it into a large ceramic salad bowl and placed it on my dining room table along with freshly toasted garlic bread.

As soon as we served ourselves healthy portions of the steaming hot dish, I poured us a couple glasses of wine and we ate and reminisced about our terrible ordeal with the bogus film company where we first met. We talked about how the wannabe producer conned us all with his phony promises of money. Evidently, somebody had reported the production company to the Federal Government because I was later contacted by someone wanting information regarding the production, but of course I said nothing because I didn't really know anything except we didn't get paid what was owed to us. They had probably left town by the time I was contacted. I think they must have known that the law was after them because I never heard from them again. I did, however, read something in a Las Vegas newspaper where they were still claiming to be casting for a movie about Marvin.

Once we ate and got settled, Zeola proceeded to light up a joint, and I turned on my tape recorder and we went to work.

Zeola started the session by making it a known fact that she knows very little about the financial issues Marvin faced with Berry Gordy. *"Only what everybody else has read in books and magazines."* But she did state that those financial squabbles that the two men were having did sometimes affect Marvin's relationship with Mr. Gordy's sister, Anna, especially after she and Marvin divorced.

Zeola stated that there were always conflicts between the two men; whether it was about the music or about Anna, or about Marvin not completing a tour or not finishing an album on time.

At that point I almost told her to 'forget it' and move on to another subject because anybody who has read anything about Marvin knows that he and Mr. Gordy had conflicts, but I did not interrupt her. Once again I had to be reminded that not only is this lady trying to tell her story about her brother, but it also appeared to be therapeutic for her. So I continued to record without interruption.

"Marvin used to say to me that he was just as talented as Berry. And I believe that he was, in his own way. But Berry was the chess master. He always won the game. They liked to play those mental games." Zeola said with a gentle 'Marvin' smile. I call it a 'Marvin smile' because in addition to the close similarity in their facial expressions, Zeola's smile was out of the ordinary

when she talked about her brother. Stories about Marvin seemed to produce an expression of pride and dignity in her face. She didn't tuck her head down toward her chest like a little girl about to be chastised by her father for speaking out. I am sure that she never realized that she was doing it, and I never mentioned it to her because I sometimes enjoyed witnessing her 'little girl' antics. She may have sold me out on completing this book, and yes, it made me mad as hell, but I hold no grudges.

"When Marvin and Anna got a divorce in 1975 the judge ordered Marvin to give all the proceeds of his next album to Anna as a settlement for their divorce, and Marvin didn't want to do it."

Zeola explained that this was another example of Marvin's problems with authority.

"He just couldn't handle being ordered to do something that he didn't want to do. I remember him asking me why he's got to give up his money to somebody else if it is his voice."

Since this album was to go to Anna, Zeola said that Marvin decided to write it about her and their relationship. Marvin recorded the album in 1977 and released it in 1978, and Zeola said that all of it was not good.

"He wrote about how she was an alcoholic, and how she couldn't have children and everything. It even included something about Berry."

After listening to Zeola describe the contents of the album, I became very curious so I decided to read the lyrics and check out her allocations because I did not remember Marvin calling Anna an alcoholic and not being able to conceive in the song 'Here My Dear'. And sure enough; after double checking the lyrics I found nothing that I felt resembled those allocations.

Here, My Dear
MARVIN GAYE

I guess I'd have to say this album is
dedicated to you.
Although perhaps you may not be happy,
this is what you want,
so I conceded.
I hope it makes you happy.
There's a lot of truth in it, babe.

I don't think I'll have many regrets, baby.
Things didn't have to be the way they was, baby.
You don't have the right to use the son of mine
to keep me in line.
One thing I can't do without
is the boy whom God gave to both of us.
I'm so happy, oh, for the son of mine.

So here it is, babe.
I hope you enjoy, reminisce, be happy,
think about the kisses and the joy.
But there were those other moments too,
the times that were cloudy and grey.
Bad.
But you taught me that was life.
May love ever protect you,
may peace come into your life.
Always think of me the way I was.
Ha, I was your baby.

This is what you wanted.
Here, dear, here it is.
Here, my dear, here it is.

Since I couldn't find anything in that song that pertained to what Zeola was suggesting, I thought maybe she meant that Marvin included those things in the over-all album, so I read the lyrics from another cut entitled WHEN DID YOU STOP LOVING ME, WHEN DID I STOP LOVING YOU.

When Did You Stop Loving Me, When Did I Stop Loving You
Marvin Gaye

You know, when you say your marriage vows, they're supposed to be for real. I mean...
if you think back about what you really said, what it's all about, honor, loving and
obeying till death do us part and all. But it shouldn't be that way, it should...it
should, it should be lies because it turns out to be lies. If you don't honor what
you said, you lie to God. The words should be changed
Ooo now as I recall, we tried a million times
Again and again and again, and that isn't all
I gave my love to you each time to make amends
Suddenly I start to realize I can't make it
Pretty birds fly away, I had to leave you for my health's sake
What to do? Make you pay, for leaving you, my fine, is to pay forever
So if a fresh new love comes in, I won't say those words again
Instead I'll say I'll try to love and protect you
With all my heart as long as you want me to baby

Ooo if I love again I'm gonna try a new way this time
Memories of the things we did; some we're proud of, some we hid
So when two people have to part, sometimes it makes them stronger
Do you remember all of the fights we had?
You say you love me with all your heart
If you ever loved me will all of your heart
You'd never take $1 million to part

I really tried, you know I tried, oh baby
Although we tried, all of those promises was nothin' but lies
I really tried, you know how I tried, we really lied, didn't we baby?
And on top of that you have scared the life, my name
But I can't understand, 'cause if you love me
How could you turn me into nothin' least
Didn't I love you good and try to take care of you?
Best I could, you were so inviting and your love was like mellow wine
Pains of love, miles of tears, after lasting for my lifetime
Broken hearts last for years and break away to the blue-day sunshine
One thing I can promise, friend: I'll never be back again
But we're not really bitter babe
I promise you all the love in the world, good love in the world
But I know you'll never be satisfied just to have me by your side
Memories haunt you all the time, I will never leave, you're mine
God judged me on His side; you've said bad things and you've lied
Still I remember some of the good things baby
Of love after dark and picnics in parks
Those are the days I'd love to get in my life
I'd rather remember, remember the joy we shared babe
I'd rather remember all the fun we had
All I ever really wanted was to love you and treat you right
All we did was fuss and fight
It don't matter baby, take a lesson from them all
I never thought I'd see the day when you'd put me through what you put
me through
You try your best, you say I gave you no rest

[Repeat and fade:]
When did you stop loving me? When did I stop loving you?

I didn't recognize much pertaining to Anna's personal
issues in that song either. So I continued to search through the
album. And when I saw a song entitled ANNA'S SONG I was
sure that I had found what I was looking for.

Anna's Song Lyrics
Marvin Gaye

This is Anna's song
I'm making love all night long,
take a bath in milk, and lay on your satin sheets
laughing smiling,(oh oh)
lay a while in,(oh oh)
chocolate mint, candy sweets

(living across the way)cross the way
(living across the way, living across the way)
this is Anna's song
(this is Anna's song, this is Anna's song)
keep on singing (loving my song)
all night long (loving my song)

oooh work so hard, see me making dollars
(never worked so hard)
I know I should for my own good, what's it her smile,
makes you so stubborn and oh
didn't you notice the snow, starting to fall
come let us sit a while, just listen
to the children laughing and running wild

Anna Anna Anna
yeah this is Anna's song hey baby hey baby
loving you all night long
let it happen again and again and again baby Anna yeah,
she's a child of the sun, lovingest one of all
mmm and this is Anna's song yeah
keep on loving me baby loving me cross the hall,
she can't do no wrong 'cos this is Anna's song
laugh and chatter to you, kiss me Anna dear

ooohhhh baby
[instrumental]
hey Anna here's your song yeah
the one that I promise baby, promise you all along
I knew all the time that I'd find the rhyme
never have a fear, here it is my dear

To my disappointment I found nothing, but I liked the song. The next one is entitled ANGER.

Anger
Marvin Gaye

Up and down my back, my spine, in my brain
It injures me, babe....

Anger, can make you old, yes it can
I said anger, can make you sick, children... oh Jesus
Anger destroys your soul
Rage, there's no room for rage in there
There's no room for rage in here
line up some place to go to be mad
It's a sin to treat your body bad

When anger really gets the best of us
We've really lost our heads
We often say a lot of things, oh darlin'
Wish we'd never said
Oh, reason is beyond control
And the things we do spite
Makes me ashamed
And I mean this, baby, makes me want to the things right

Someday soon I hope and pray like Jesus

181

I'll reach that wiser age
Hope I will learn I really never never profit
>From things I do in rage

One more time-anger, more anger
When it's flaming hot
Anger burns to the bitter end
Know what I'm talkin' 'bout
When it cools I find out too late
I have lost at love, love, love, dear friend
I said, anger will make you sick,
children, oh Jesus
Anger destroys your soul

I ain't gonna let you get the best of me, babe
I'm gonna go somewhere and cool
This is not the way my head's supposed to be, babe
You've got me feelin' like some silly fool
But I know a real nice place where I can go
And feel the way I'm supposed to feel

I don't want to be mad at nobody
I don't want to be feelin' bad
Up and down my back, my spine, in my brain
It injures me, babe

Anger, can make you old, yes it can
I said anger will make you sick, children, oh Jesus
Anger destroys your soul
Anger
Anger

That was a great song about 'anger' but not about Anna or Mr. Gordy that I could recognize. Another song on the HERE MY DEAR album is SPARROW of which I already know the lyrics because I reflected back on the incident where the little dove visited me while writing an earlier chapter. So I decided to move on to another song from the album HERE MY DEAR entitled:

"You Can Leave, But It's Going to Cost You"
Marvin Gaye

I remember like it was yesterday
we were over Gwen's, and we were trying one more time to make amends
Oh yes we were
Suddenly it occurred to me it did not matter
whether I was mad at her
or she was at me
Nawww understanding my condition I must surely be a wishing
and a hoping to be free
Chorus
She said... You can leave, but it's going to cost you ....
She said... You can leave, but it's going to cost you.
She said ... you can lea..ve, but it's gonna cost you dearly
you....can leave but it gonna cost you how dearly
Ooohhhhhhhh
Sometimes my eyes were red as fire
Intoxicated ...
Sometimes the spirit was moving on me
I had to fight to defend my life
I'm gone, I'm gone, I'm gone(get use to it baby)
I'm gone, I'm, gone, I'm gone(get use to it baby)

You use to say that I was a gorgeous hunk of man...
that didn't help me baby Ah...when you were on the stand

Well, the lyrics about going to court seemed to get pretty close.

"A Funky Space Reincarnation"
Marvin Gaye

Two thousand and seventy three, two thousand and eighty four, two
thousand and ninety three, light years ahead you and me gone be
getting down on a space bed.....we gone get married in June....we
gonna be getting down on the moon, light years interplanetary forms
on the get down star wars interplanetary funk......still getting down
......music won't have no race only face... peaceful face.... all the time
on this trip stuck inside my mother ship I can tell on your face that
you really wanna stay SPACE FUNKY SPACE........peaceful space..
certain place wait till I feel cool.....HEY BABY lets get in the
groove.........Don't you look like somebody I met a long time ago I
know I ain't ever met you though oooh you look like I've been
knowing you for a thousand years gosh ooh I don't know what's
happening you know I'm really involved but I been checking you out
you know uh getting some other reaction seems to me though that we
been together here we supposed to be together COME ON BABY
let's go peace loving and check out this new smoke naw this thing I
got it ain't classified as dope smoke I got from venus have had it all
week its getting old come on and try this new thing with me baby
...too cold....come on now baby lets take off clean get in this sin
machine and rock it rock it rock it rock it hey little baby let's
magnetize magnets makes the love rise baby oooh sugar lets get some
more why do I feel like I've been....with ......you .....before shoot me
baby with the creator lots of peace and lots of fun......everybody he

184

*created having lots of fun lets move the party over to star 1
.......alright everybody we're moving now to come in for our landing
here PLUTO all of you who are in group A send you over to the
pludatarium to get plutotized know you can dig that and the rest of
the group B I know ya'll gone have a ball BUT HEY little Miss Bird
song come here YOU FOLLOW ME......come on baby come on down
come on baby come on down (LETS RAZZMATAZZ AND ALL
THAT JAZZ LETS TOUCH EACH OTHER LETS TOUCH
EACH OTHER LETS RAZZMATAZZ AND ALL THAT JAZZ)
{Repeated over COME ON BABY over and over} come on lets say
what we mean put our hearts into the real machine . say YEAH say
Yes......STOP........well its been a fantastic trip (ya'll cut it out)
Come back next week player ITS FUNKYFUL everybody get your
heads together be right here on time all we gotta say is TIME FOR
THE COUNTDOWN we gonna count down zack we going you
ready? 1 fun 2 you 3 me 4 more 5 no jive 6 no tricks 7 we in heaven
8 everything is straight 9 FINE..... TEEEEEN! next week we'll do it
again! OWWWW!!!!!!!*

Nope, I couldn't find anything in those lyrics either.

"Falling in Love Again"
Marvin Gaye

*In this life....of....happiness and sadness
when you've lost....out on love...
and it all...ends up in madness
and you say....Love....please go away don't torture me, night and day
then someone real.....someone who feel comes in.*

chorus
Now I'm falling in love again

185

I'm falling in love again
I'm falling in love all over
I'm falling in love again
I, I found somebody , she says she love me
I'm falling in love again, falling in love again, falling in love
Once again........Hey baby
She's pretty, outside and in...
She's so wonderful.....I tried not to let my heart step in.......
But what to do...baby...what could I......do......
when somebody real comes in.....
Someone who feel......comes in........

chorus
Now I'm falling in love again
I'm falling in love again
I found somebody , she says she love me
I'm falling in love again....awwww beautiful woman
falling in love again, falling in love again, falling in love

Music plays
I.........Love........YOU..........

I could not find the lyrics for the song entitled, "Is That Enough", but odds are that if nothing existed in any of these other songs I doubt if it exists in that one. I just couldn't make out where Marvin sings about Anna's personal issues. Maybe it was the effects of the weed this time, or maybe I'm just not interpreting the lyrics properly. Maybe everybody should judge for themselves.

Also, I saw nothing that I could interpret as an insinuation against Berry Gordy. So once again, I can't ask her about it, which frustrates me because she was so very adamant about her chain of events but this particular event does not seem to have occurred.

It is my understanding that she has recently been associated with live productions about what some critics have described as very amateurish plays about her famous brother. As we are all aware, we cannot always depend on what critics say, so I hope that her productions are a bit different than the parties that I have witnessed that were supposedly on Marvin's behalf. It is so unfortunate that nobody has given Marvin's legacy the professional celebration he so deserves. There are rumors of motion pictures and documentaries to be released about his legacy. Maybe one of them will honor him deservingly.

After Marvin finished the album for Anna, Zeola said that he couldn't think of what to call it. Marvin told her that while he was in the studio, he was trying to think of a name and all he could come up with was the word, 'Here.' She said that he kept saying *"Here... Here..."*

"He said he was so angry that he had to give the money to Anna that he said things like 'Here, Bitch!' But he knew that he couldn't use that because he really did love Anna, and it was not his intent to hurt her. He told me that Dick Gregory was there at that time and said, '...My Dear.' And Marvin loved it. So, Marvin said, 'My Dear... Here, My Dear!' And that became the name of the album, 'Here, My Dear.' Unlike what Dick Gregory said about taking total credit for naming the cover; he only added to the name. That was all. I guess everybody wants to have a little piece of the credit, even the good guys."

I think that she might be correct on this allocation because I read something similar to this a few years back.

Zeola said that Marvin liked the album cover. She explained that if you look at it you will see that a man's hand is reaching out to a woman's hand. She said that this depicts Marvin giving Anna the album.

"But what is even more interesting is that on Marvin's side of the album cover there are indications of conflict. Beside and around the man's hand are pictures of the devil, a piano, a dead rose and a bottle of poison. On Anna's side there are beautiful roses, jewels and furs. The concept was beautiful and the album was awesome."

Zeola said that when Marvin called Anna in to listen to it, he told her that if there was anything in there that offended her or that she felt was an embarrassment to her that he would take it out. But when Anna listened to the album, Zeola said that being the cool way that Anna is, she chuckled at the lyrics. And the one that won her heart the most was the song named, ANNA. That song, according to Zeola, took care of everything that Marvin wanted to say. And she loved it. So the two of them were okay with the lyrics, but Zeola said that Berry wasn't.

"He was upset because Marvin had said some things about him that he didn't like."

Well, I didn't see anything bad, but maybe there were some subliminal messages in there that I couldn't detect. I suppose that will be left up to the reader.

The album didn't make very much money. Zeola felt that Motown did not promote it like they usually did. She said that she believes that Berry was put in a really strange position because he was damned if he did, and damned if he didn't. The album was promised to Anna, but Zeola claims that it contained some really messy stuff, so Zeola was sure that Berry was troubled by the whole idea of releasing it. But being a businessman, and he had to get Anna's money, Zeola said that he released it.

"I am sure he was just about ready to get rid of Marvin too for telling all of his sister's business."

Chapter
15

IN OUR LIFETIME

1981

According to Zeola, Marvin did not know that the soundtrack to the album, IN OUR LIFETIME had been brought back to the United States without his permission. As far as he was concerned, she said that he was still working on it.

"You can actually hear Marvin's voice humming on it because he hadn't finished it yet." Zeola said. She went on to explain that a deadline had passed on the soundtrack, and Mr. Gordy wanted his money, so the guys took what they had back to the States, and the next thing Marvin knew the album had been released unfinished. When Marvin found this out he was totally pissed. He demanded to know how Motown got it, and who took it.

"I don't know exactly who told Marvin that the conga player and the bass player copied the track and took it, and I don't know if he did anything to them for doing it, but after that, Marvin rebelled royally against Motown. Marvin told me that he wasn't doing shit for Berry Gordy or Motown ever again. And he didn't. He was like that. He was very stubborn. And because of this he became very depressed. The tracks weren't even finished. He did not want something put out there that wasn't complete. Marvin was a perfectionist when it came to his work."

Zeola told me that Marvin compared this to an architect who has drawn up his plans and suddenly somebody comes in and changes it without his knowledge. She said that Marvin told her that he felt that IN OUR LIFETIME was his baby, and nobody should have had the right to alter it without his permission. And that was the last time he recorded anything for Motown Records, to her knowledge.

"Marvin was really depressed. IN OUR LIFETIME wasn't doing too good. I truly believe that it was because it didn't have

Marvin's blessings. I believe that that album would have had at least five or six songs on there that would have been number one hits if Marvin had only had the opportunity to finish them the way he wanted to finish them. And if it had been released the way Marvin wanted it released."

At age forty-two while living in London, England and down on his luck, Marvin was approached by a young and enthusiastic small-time promoter and long time fan named Freddy Cousaert. Marvin still had his son Bubbie with him so Freddy Cousaert invited the two of them to come and stay with him and his family in their beautiful home in Ostend, Belgium off the North Sea. This obviously worked well for Marvin. He was reported to have said that he truly loved the clean air and picturesque seaside.

I visited Ostend in 1991 and fell in love with the fresh air, great little cafes and wonderful restaurants and boutiques lined up along the picturesque seaside.

Marvin and Bubbie had practically become members of the Cousaert family and Marvin seemed to be on the rebound to recovery. Unfortunately, that did not last forever.

Around 1981 Marvin was all set to come home to America and return to work, and with the help of Cousaert and his long time attorney, Curtis Shaw, he finally got out of the Motown contract and began looking for a new deal, which he found with Columbia Records. However, it did not happen overnight. Marvin's reputation of cocaine abuse in London had followed him, and nobody wanted to deal with him.

Formally an executive at Capital Records, Attorney Larkin Arnold was quickly becoming a big department head over the Black music department at Columbia Records (CBS) and expressed interest in Marvin. But he had to convince the execs at CBS that Marvin was ready.

"On one of Larkin's interviews on television he talked about how he had been told that Marvin was all drugged out and sad-looking over in Belgium. But Larkin said that when he got there he was surprised to see how well Marvin was doing. He said that Marvin was not on drugs at all. Larkin said that Marvin seemed very healthy and in a great state of mind. He said that Marvin was running and energetic and ready to work. So a proposal was made to Marvin that would get him out of his contract with Motown, and the deal was a good one. Marvin's first project for CBS turned out to be SEXUAL HEALING.

Marvin told Zeola that even though CBS bought him out of the Motown contract, Berry Gordy still got a great deal of money out of it. *"I don't know a lot about that. I only know what Marvin told me."* Zeola admitted. She said that Marvin told her that he was very glad to be out of the deal with Berry and Motown Records.

"Little did he know that the worse was yet to come. Somehow, after SEXUAL HEALING, Marvin went from his contract with CBS to a contract with the devil."

CHAPTER
16

LONDON

"I think it was 1978, before Marvin got involved with promoters. I remember nearing the end of a tour in England and the promoters had set up a private concert for Princess Margaret because we were told that she was totally in love with Marvin. She was one of the jetsetters at that time. We were supposed to be at the concert at 7:00 pm and time was just flying by, but Marvin was having problems with the promoters because they didn't want to give him the money to pay the band. Back in those days Marvin's band was one of the highest paid bands that anybody had. They were making about twelve to fifteen hundred dollars a week plus per diem. Plus, he kept them happy with drugs. So Marvin decided that he was not going unless the promoter gave the band their money. The promoters said that they weren't going to pay that kind of money, so Marvin said that he wasn't going on. In the meantime Princess Margaret was waiting, and didn't know the reason for the hold up."

I really enjoyed Zeola when she talked about Marvin. Not only would her eyes light up at times, but she sometimes got so animated that I could almost see Marvin in her expressions. She had a great way of telling her story even though I sometimes questioned the accuracy of her dates.

"Finally, the British promoter called and told Princess Margaret that Marvin would not be able to make it. Well, she got upset about it and had her lady-in-waiting call the hotel, and I answered the telephone. She told me who she was and that Princess Margaret was really looking forward to Marvin performing for the court. I asked her if I could talk to Marvin and call her back and she said, 'Yes.' So I went to Marvin and told him that the lady-in-waiting had called and that Princess Margaret really wanted to see him. Marvin told me to call her back and tell her that he would come. So when I called her back and told her what Marvin had said. They sent Marvin about ten or fifteen royal cars to pick us up at the hotel. By the time we got there it must have been about eleven o'clock at night and

Princess Margret had left, but Marvin performed for the rest of the court. The very next morning all of the European newspapers read: MARVIN SNUBBS PRINCESS.

We couldn't believe it. Of course we found out that over there you just don't do anything against the royal family. So Marvin had to go on all the radio stations and television shows and attempt to explain what happened. In the meantime the promoters never did pay the band. Marvin ended up paying them. And because of all that confusion we all ended up picketing in front of the promoter's building, yelling that they were unfair.

After we picketed that day, Marvin had to send everybody home with money out of his pocket. I'm not sure if Motown was involved or not. Again, I was too young to know all of the particulars. All I know is that Marvin started sending four members of the band home at a time. After that we had nothing to do but party and get high. In the meantime, we were all living in this big four leveled flat, and we were kicking it with my mom and two of her friends who had come with her. They cooked enough food for everybody. We were having a good time.

That was the first time I had ever been on a picket line, and it was a weird experience for all of us, being Americans picketing on European soil, but we got our point across to them."

I was also informed by another source that a lady named Jewel, one of Marvin's oldest friends and confidant, was also instrumental in finally persuading Marvin to perform that night in London. I suppose we will never know who was actually responsible for getting him there, and it really isn't that important. Maybe it took both parties and possibly a few others to finally convince the super star to cooperate. It seems like there were many times in which Marvin needed a little friendly persuasion to do the right thing. I suppose the moods of a true genius can be quite difficult to deal with at times.

"*Eventually the Europeans realized the truth and Marvin was once again well-loved over there, and of course he sent a very formal apology to Princess Margaret. If I am not mistaken, he sent her some flowers, and she responded with a thank you. She was very happy that he came anyway and performed for the court even though she missed the performance.*"

CHAPTER
17

SEXUAL HEALING 1983

Entertainment Group was a management company that worked in conjunction with one of the largest chains of theatrical venues in the United States. Zeola said that one of Jan's friends apparently knew the owners of these companies and arranged a meeting between them and Marvin. Marvin told Zeola that they wanted to promote a tour for him, but they told him that he had to make sure to complete the tour. They told him that they owned a lot of super stars and would not tolerate anything less than his best.

"I will never forget Marvin telling me that the owner of these theatres told him that this would be his last hurrah. I asked Marvin what that meant. It sounded like the man must have been very old, and that this would be his last booking, but Marvin said that the owner was talking about it being Marvin's last hurrah."

Marvin also told Zeola that the owner said that Marvin would be the last Black person that the owner will ever manage. He said that his other Black person was Sammy Davis Jr. Marvin accepted the offer and his final tour was set in motion. When the Sexual Healing Tour was booked Zeola said that Marvin was sure that he was finally back on track.

"But what Marvin didn't know was that he had just made a deal with the devil."

The tour started in San Diego in the 70's, and by the time it got to New York Zeola said that it was a mess. She said that Marvin was booked to perform the next day at Radio City Music Hall, but Al Sharpton had already formed a picket line out front charging the music hall with discrimination against Black Artists.

I asked Zeola for more details about the discrimination charges because I couldn't understand why Marvin would be booked there during that time, but she was unable to go into details. I attempted to look it up on the internet, but there must have been hundreds of incidents where Al Sharpton has picked Radio City Music Hall and none of them seemed to fit the time frame, nor did any of them mention Marvin's appearance. I am sure the information is there. I just couldn't find it. I get so frustrated when searching the internet. I suppose I'm still ole-school.

"So, in order to perform the next day Marvin had to cross that line, and he wasn't happy about that but he had made a deal not to miss any shows with the new promoters, and he knew that he could not get out of it. So, Marvin met with Al Sharpton that night to discuss the reason for the picket signs."

I asked Zeola what they had discussed, but she wasn't sure of that either.

"I don't know too much about what happened in Marvin's room that night between him and Al Sharpton except that I remember that there were a lot of people coming and going from Marvin's room, and none of them looked familiar to Robin and me. We just stayed in our room and looked out the door periodically to see if anything crazy was going on. But everything was okay."

Marvin later told Zeola that he and Al Sharpton came to an agreement that Marvin would do something for Al Sharpton in the near future if he let the show go on. So she said that Marvin did cross the picket line and perform the next night and everything went okay.

"Marvin even broke the record for attendance at Radio City Music Hall."

The next morning Zeola said that she could hear Marvin yelling that his cocaine had been stolen. She said that he woke everybody up.

"It turned out that on the night before when Marvin came off the stage and wanted his cocaine, Jan told him that Robin and I had it."

200

Many times when they were on the road Zeola said that Marvin would get a suite and put her in one of the rooms so that he could keep an eye on her.

"So Jan came to my door and asked for the coke. I told her that I didn't have it. I reminded her that she had given Robin and me a little of it, but that she had taken the rest of it with her when she left."

By now Zeola said that Marvin had gotten really upset because he wanted his stuff and Jan was saying that she left it with Zeola, and Zeola was saying that Jan was lying.

"So then Marvin had to make a decision as to who to believe. So he called court with Robin, Jan, and her friends, Barbara, Denise, and myself."

Zeola started telling me how Jan, Barbara and Denise were the same ones who had lots of orgies together, so I asked her if she and Robin participated, and she said, *"No."*

"Apparently I presented my case pretty good because I asked Marvin why I would take the coke when I had no friends with me that needed that much stuff, plus Marvin always gave me what I wanted."

That night after Marvin dismissed everybody and they all went to their rooms, Zeola said that she and Robin started trying to analyze the situation.

"We were always trying to figure out shit. We figured that Jan was about to be sent home because she and Marvin had been arguing earlier about something, so it made more sense for her to want to take the coke with her."

But before they could figure this one out Zeola said that something happened that answered everything.

"Marvin threw Jan her fur coat because he was sending her home when he noticed that it seemed very heavy for a fox fur. It turned out that Jan had cut the lining of her coat and had stuffed the

cocaine that she had accused me of taking in the lining of her coat. Well, Marvin got really mad that time, and he acted real ugly. They had a terrible fight that night."

Zeola said that the Gayes were at it again.

"Finally, Marvin put Jan out and called her and her friends all kinds of names and then apologized to Robin and me. But you know what? That was almost fun to me because the whole game of wit was so deep in the room that night and I had won. It was just Robin and me against everybody else. Her friends were all against us, and Marvin was even leaning towards her side for a minute or two. Marvin had a lot of sessions like that, but I liked that particular night because Robin and I had to really work at making our case strong, and we succeeded."

After that, Zeola said that Robin went home, and the next tour was in Florida, and she said that Jan came back.

Once again, a whole network of confusion was going on behind Marvin's back with the promoters, but Zeola said that she never got a chance to explore what all of the confusion was about.

The next tour was in Houston, Texas, and Zeola said that Marvin decided this time to give the cocaine to her to hold because he didn't trust Jan. *"He decided that if anybody wanted cocaine they had to get it from me,"* Zeola boasted.

By this time Zeola said that she needed help again.

"Not only did I have my usual responsibilities but now I was in charge of the cocaine as well. So once again I called on my dear friend Robin to come back out again."

When Robin said that she couldn't come right then Zeola said that she was disappointed, but knew that Robin had a family, and would come as soon as she could.

"So we headed out to Sunrise Florida where Marvin was instructed by the promoters to just relax and do nothing."

Jan and Marvin had fought at almost every hotel they stayed at, according to Zeola.

"Practically every night they were breaking windows and furniture and shit." Zeola remembered hearing the people say, *"The Gayes are at it again."*

Zeola said that the management team thought that Marvin should take a break from Jan so they didn't want Jan to go to Florida, but Marvin let her come anyway. And by the time everybody arrived in Sunrise, Florida, Zeola said that even Marvin had decided that Jan needed to go because of the fighting.

"While we were in Florida Marvin asked to be taken to the hospital because he wasn't feeling well. He had been tooting cocaine constantly from May through June and it was taking its toll on him. The promoters didn't want to say that cocaine was the reason Marvin was hospitalized so they said that it was due to exhaustion. They knew that the media would have had a field day if it were due to drugs."

Zeola said that Marvin told her that nobody was to come in to see him except his bodyguard and her.

"I told him that Jan was outside and wanted to visit him, but he insisted that he didn't want her in the room. So when I told her that he had said that she should go home because he didn't want to see her, she broke down and started crying. She kept saying how much she loved him, so I went back upstairs and told him that she was crying and that she said that she loved him and wanted to see him."

Well, Marvin told the bodyguard, who was one of the management people, that he didn't want to see Jan, Zeola said. *"And the bodyguard, who was so cool, handled it immediately. He sent Jan home. He was the best. Not only was he a fine-looking Jewish man, but also everything that he did was done in a smooth way. I really admired him. I always felt safe whenever he was around."*

Marvin spent a couple of days in the hospital while the doctors tried to fix his nose, but Zeola said that there wasn't too much they could do for him. The cocaine had practically eaten through Marvin's nostrils. The doctors said that only time would heal his nose.

"Robin met us at the next airport in Michigan. We were all glad to see each other. And most of all, we were glad that Jan had been sent home so that we could all have a little peace of mind because Marvin had started to become really paranoid about Jan. He had found out that she and her mom had taken out this insurance policy on him and he didn't like it."

By the time we completed the show in Michigan, Zeola said that Marvin had graduated to premos, which is another way of doing cocaine.

"Robin called them coco puffs. Robin always said that she called them coco puffs because she used to say that you've got coco (cocaine) and you puff on it. So she called them coco puffs. But I always called them cocktails. I don't remember when I first started calling them that, but I always did, and Marvin never questioned it."

The cocktails didn't do the damage that snorting did to Marvin's nose, but Marvin did seem to become even more paranoid than ever, Zeola said.

"When we got to the airport in Michigan Marvin had become so paranoid that he insisted that we dump all the cocaine on the floor of the limousine and smash it. Well, Andre, Robin and me said "To hell with that!" We were not about to waste all that good shit. So we all decided that we would tell Marvin that we threw it away, but we were not about to get rid of any of it."

Zeola said that one of them passed the cocaine on to the next one, and the next one passed it on, and they all said, *"Yeah, alright, we threw it away."* By the time they got to the next town the drugs had worn off a little bit and Marvin was thinking straight, and Zeola said that's when he wanted more cocaine.

"Now we're in a new city and we don't know anybody with drugs. Of course later on we would get contacts, but right now we don't have anything. So by now Marvin really thinks that we have nothing. Marvin looked at me and asked me if I had anything, and I told him "No." But he knew me so well that he knew that I was lying. Finally, I pulled it out and gave it to Robin so that she could make the cocktail aka coco puff for Marvin. I remember that once he found out that we hadn't thrown any of it away, he was so tickled."

Zeola remembered once while they were all staying at the Red Lion Inn in Detroit, Michigan some real shaky dudes talked Marvin into coming back to their house.

"Even our bodyguard was nervous because these were some straight up gangsters."

Well, Zeola said that Marvin was having a natural ball. The owner of the house took them to his basement and they were all talking and laughing and drinking and having a good time.

"We were just kicking it in a typically laid out east coast basement, shooting pool and shit. At this point we hadn't seen a lot of cocaine or anything like that."

Finally the owner invited them upstairs, and when they got up there, Zeola said that they saw more Black folks than they had ever seen in their lives in one house.

"There was one room where everybody had to put their guns, and another room where there was nothing in there but cocaine. Well, we almost panicked. Marvin was just sitting in the middle of

the room while everybody was passing around plates filled with mounds of cocaine. Marvin was loving it. He was sitting there with a straw and was going to town with those plates of cocaine. Every time somebody passed a plate Marvin took a snort of it."

Zeola said that Marvin knew these guys from his Motown days, but they had never seen anything like this and they just couldn't handle it.

"So Robin told Marvin that her stomach ached and she wanted to go home. But we all wanted to leave that place that night. We were almost in a panicked state of mind even though everybody there treated us in a nice way. But all we could think about was what if another gang busted in, or maybe the police would come. Plus, cocaine makes you paranoid and we had already done our share of that as well as doing a gig that night, and we needed some down time."

Robin kept nudging me about the room with all the guns. She kept saying, *"Sweetsie, look at all them guns over there! We gotta get outta here! What if somebody goes berserk and start shooting? We are gonna all be dead! We gotta get outta here!"*

So because Marvin sometimes listens to his body guard Andre, Zeola and Robin told him that they wanted to get out of there.

"We told Andre that there were too many guns up in there, and we reminded him that the place could get raided and shit."

Well, even though Andre was a tough ex-pro football player from Tampa, Zeola said that he was kinda scary about that whole thing too, and he wanted to get out of there as well. So he told Marvin that they should leave, but Marvin didn't want to go.

"Marvin came over to us and told all of us to calm down. He tried to assure us that everything was cool and that we would be leaving shortly, but not right that minute. That's when Robin

repeated to Marvin that her stomach ached, and he started cracking up laughing. But Robin didn't let up. She kept telling him that she wanted to go home. Robin even considered throwing up in order to get us out of there. But nothing worked that night. We did not leave the house until Marvin got ready to leave."

In the meantime Zeola said that the three of them just hung together and waited for Marvin. *"Andre did not leave our side. I think that he was about as scared as Robin and me."*

By the time they got to the show in Detroit the next day Zeola said that there was a lot of chaos going on. It turned out that some disc jockey named Butterball wanted to be the Master of Ceremonies instead of allowing Marvin's valet and MC, Gorgeous George to do it. Well, Marvin said, *"No."* So Gorgeous George did the show.

After the shows they often times listened to tapes of the shows. And on that particular show they all listened together. Robin pointed out that Gorgeous George was saying something that wasn't cool. She said, "Marvin, listen to this shit." On the tape Gorgeous George was saying, *"Marvin Gaye! Fabulous Entertainer!"* And then Zeola said that he whispered, *"Red Lion Inn, Room ...."* She said that Gorgeous George was giving out his room number so that the girls would know where to come after the show. This way they would have to do sexual favors for him and maybe he would get them introduced to Marvin.

"Marvin got so mad he didn't know what to do. He called Gorgeous George in and laid his ass out. Marvin did everything short of firing George. But he didn't do that because over all Gorgeous George was very loyal to Marvin. He always made sure that Marvin was taken care of in spite of this sexual thing. If need be, he would even wash Marvin's socks out by hand if we were somewhere that Marvin's things couldn't get cleaned."

Unfortunately, Zeola said that Marvin balled George out in front of Robin and her, and George looked at the two of them in disgust because he had figured out that they must have told on him. After that Zeola said that he was a bit more distant to them.

"Now Robin and I had one more person that didn't like us. Gerald and Andre were already angry with us because they were Marvin's security and Marvin had started listening to more of what we had to say rather than them. Needless to say, we weren't very popular with any of Marvin's immediate staff."

The next gig was in Murrayville Indiana, and Zeola said that it was a beautiful place. "The hotel lobby was literally filled with sand like being on a beach. And right next door was the venue. It was a fantastic place. But was not about to be great for Robin and me."

After that incident, Zeola claimed that George, Gerald and Andre plotted against Robin and her so that they would get sent home.

Marvin had set a routine whereas before each show Zeola said she had to give him a cayenne pepper, honey and lemon drink and Robin had to make him a drink of parsley, banana and pineapple juice and if she didn't put his make up on him and massage his feet and he didn't get his premo, his whole performance would get thrown off. *"We also had to make sure that his rum was in his dressing room. So in order to make sure all of these things happened we would already be dressed so that we could concentrate on Marvin's needs. We always had to make sure that the hotel had placed a blender in his dressing room as well as the proper fruit so that we could make the drinks."*

Zeola said that Gorgeous George, Gerald and Andre knew that this was Marvin's routine. So on this particular day nobody called to wake them up.

"We slept right through the overture and Marvin was freaking out. So now Andre casually comes and knocks on our door and tells us that Marvin is hot because we're not there. It was almost as if he had a smirk on his face as he watched us rush around bumping into each other like frantic chickens trying to put our clothes on."

Zeola thought, *"Thank God the venue is next door and we can get there through the under ground tunnel."* but they still didn't make it on time. She said that Marvin had to go on stage without everything except his makeup. Gorgeous George did his makeup.

Marvin was mad as hell when he got off that stage. Zeola said that he yelled, *"I don't want to hear it because I'm paying you to be somewhere and you're not there!"*

Well, Zeola said that they apologized over and over and tried to convince Marvin that they were set up. She said that they told him how nobody called to wake them up and how Gorgeous George, Andre and Gerald were mad at them for telling on them.

"Finally, we talked enough to Marvin that we convinced him that it was a setup. It was a hard talk but he didn't send us home."

Zeola said that she believes that Marvin knew what was going on because he liked to play psychological games. She said that he liked to pit people against each other.

"When you pit people up against each other you expose them. So now Robin and me knew that we were not in good standing with anybody. Gorgeous George, Andre and Gerald were okay now because they had gotten their revenge and Marvin was okay with us, but not exactly the same as before. And we knew that more than likely we would be put in this position again and again until the three guys would make it so that Marvin had to send us home."

So finally Zeola's favorite person, the Jewish body guard from the promoters came to the venue and Robin suggested that they talk to him about this, and Zeola agreed. So they waited until Marvin went on stage, which meant that Gorgeous George and Andre and Gerald would all be busy for at least an hour and a half. They pulled the guard aside in a little room and told him everything, including how nobody woke them up, and how George was giving room numbers out and everything.

"He listened and told us not to worry about anything. He assured us that he would handle everything, and he did because from that point on things went so smooth for everybody. And for the first time we didn't feel like we were just a part of the woodwork. Our voices had been heard."

I asked Zeola if that Jewish guard that she always talked about was really one of the lead promoters, and she said, "No." She insisted that he just worked for the top man. She finally mentioned the name of that person, but I would rather not repeat it. I'm not sure if she was giving me the right name or not. I just chose not to put it in writing.

The next tour was in Chicago where Zeola said that they met a notorious militant group who called themselves 'The Magnificent something-or-other.' She couldn't remember the rest of their names. She said that the group had a problem with where Marvin was performing. And even though she is sure that the cocaine played a big part in their paranoia, she said that they were all petrified of these people. I never got the chance to find out if the group of militants was African American, but the word, militant, and the fact that this took place back in the 80's, leads me to believe that they were of the Black race.

Murrayville, Indiana and Chicago are right next to each other and Zeola said that the gangs in Chicago were just as scary as the ones over in Murrayville.

"To me they appeared to be much more deadly than the gangs out here on the west coast. They didn't talk a lot like we're accustomed to. Living here on the west coast it's all talk. The east coast seemed to be all action. So we were scared of all of them. I mainly remember their eyes. They were piercing and cold."

Zeola said that she was glad that they got out of there alive.

A lot of displeasure was expressed about the writer, David Ritz. Zeola claimed that David took credit for writing the song SEXUAL HEALING, but she says that Marvin told her that David Ritz did not write it. She said that he only suggested the word 'Healing' *"And now he is trying to take credit for writing the song!"* Zeola blurted out. There weren't very many times during our writing sessions that Zeola got this emotional. Short of Marvin's death, I felt that this outburst was up there with the best of them.

According to Zeola, David and Marvin also had words about a book that David had written about Marvin that angered Marvin. Zeola remembered that Marvin told David Ritz *"Fuck you. You can't write a fucking thing about me."* Zeola then presented a question to me. She asked, *"How is he going to talk about the 80's and he wasn't even around?"* Well, I told her that I didn't know how to answer her question because I had not read anything that David Ritz had written at that time about Marvin. I also told her that I didn't think that it would be very wise to put David Ritz is this book, but she insisted.

"Marvin kept repeating the word Sexual, Sexual and David said the word, 'Healing. Healing would be good.' David said. But now he's taking credit for writing the lyrics. All he gave was one word, and he gets money for that because there is nobody here to dispute him. David Ritz talked Motown into putting his name on stuff." Zeola was angry.

211

She told of an incident when David was on tour with Marvin, and had his written material about Marvin with him. She said that David would sit in the room with Marvin and her, and Marvin would tell him things just to see David's reaction.

"And then when David would leave we would crack up laughing because of the shit Marvin would tell him. He might tell David that he dressed up like a woman just to see David's reactions. He loved doing shit like that."

Zeola said that both she and Marvin really disliked David. She said that David referred to her a lot in his book, but she said that you won't find one quote from her because Marvin instructed her not to talk to David. I'll bet that Marvin never realized that David would write in a book that he dressed up like a woman, or he would not have told him that. It seems that that joke came back to bite Marvin. I suppose that is partly why he was so angry with David (if he really was angry with David) but I can't be sure because I wasn't there.

"Marvin said that he didn't care what happens that I shouldn't talk to David Ritz. And my mother and my sister would not have talked to David if they had known that he would not keep his promises, but they needed the money. And they had no idea that he would twist around a lot of things that my mother said. All these people who are dead can't defend themselves, and nobody else has stepped forward to defend my family's honor. So people are going to believe what this mother-fucker wrote. So it's time I did that. I'm tired of my family being shit on. It's time to set the record straight. I've got to give it up. Fuck 'em. Fuck everybody. These people were all out of line. And how dare they say that Marvin didn't have a family that he loved. People have made comments that we were a stumbling block for him, and that hurts me deeply."

Zeola went on to say that Marvin loved his family.

"My mother has said many times to the press how much Marvin loved us. Marvin loved his family. People are jealous. Marvin made it comfortable for us where I didn't have to work a nine to five, and my mother didn't have to clean people houses anymore and we had a house, but we didn't have the best. What was wrong with that? We didn't have a million dollar home up in the hills, or anything like that. He just made us comfortable. And these were things that he wanted to do."

Zeola went on to say that if he didn't want to do the things that he did, he wouldn't have done them.

"And people faulted us for that. But they were the ones who had their hands out, begging and shit. But Marvin was my brother. He was my brother. And nobody knew him or loved him more than his family."

I remained quiet while Zeola continued to vent. I felt that she needed this moment because it was obvious that she had a lot of anger and frustrations that she needed to get out of her system. But at the same time I was waiting to hear what the family had done for Marvin, and I did not hear anything about that.

"Did it make sense that the two women that Marvin married were jealous of me? Just because my brother loved me? They are the ones who slept with him. And they sure as hell got more money than I did. What I think they may not have gotten was being Marvin best friend. I was Marvin's best friend. Maybe that's what they wanted from him. But I never treated them bad, but I wasn't going to let them shit on me either. I speak up. I'm a Gay. I was always cordial to them. Yes, I could have played them. I could have played the fuck out of them, and Marvin wouldn't have said a word, but I didn't. So, yeah, he loved me. And yeah, he was my best friend."

Zeola said that her family treated everybody with love. She said that they watched their kids and everything.

"Now my father could be mean when he wanted to, but overall he just demanded respect. I don't know why, but people just didn't like us. I love my family. I don't think any of us went out of our way to drain anybody dry, or live in big houses, or buy big cars. We are just normal people. Marvin was normal. He just happened to have a talent that people loved. A talent that God gave him. And we were able to enjoy life a little bit. I don't think that's wrong. But people did. And they still treat us like that. I don't understand it. I don't really give a fuck anymore though. Nobody's doing anything for me. What I don't understand though, is why my family is still struggling. We live one paycheck from being homeless, like most people. And all these people who have lied about Marvin and exploited him are making big bucks off him. I don't understand right now, but maybe some day I will. I'm more hurt that bitter."

After Zeola made those statements I was feeling a bit bad because I too have been finding fault with the family. I too feel that the support that Marvin needed was not there. I believe that none of them knew how to be supportive. They only seemed to know how to receive, and that is what was so unfortunate.

Zeola said that she could see it if they were people who mistreated others, but she said that they weren't like that, and I believe that there was no mistreatment intended. But no support seemed to be considered either.

"My kids are great. My nieces and nephew are great. I've got a beautiful grand child, my son-in-law is a great person, and my sister-in-law is good. We have a nice family. We're not in jail or anything."

When a star is placed in Hollywood on the Hollywood Walk of Fame Zeola said that the family usually gets a replica of that star.

"Well, nobody gave us a star. It went to his ex wife and Berry Gordy. We didn't get anything. That bothered me deeply. So, I've been quiet too long. No more nice guys. I'm tired. I've seen and heard so much stuff about my brother that wasn't true. I'm tired of seeing and hearing people say anything they want to say, and profiting from it, while my family suffers financially."

Ironically, Zeola followed this heart wrenching speech by saying how much she wanted this book to sell because she thinks that the rest of her family deserves to be happy that they had a brother as beautiful as Marvin was. Yet, it only took her ex-sister-in-law, somebody whom she claimed to have disliked intensely, to offer a few measly dollars not to write the book, and she agreed to do it; all for the almighty dollar. I think this makes my point.

CHAPTER
18

PEACE

"*Marvin wanted to die,*" Zeola stated. She said that he was unhappy and often times spoke of suicide.

"*He was so unhappy. He said that his battles seemed endless, and he just wanted a little peace in his life. He had to deal with the underground syndicate, the IRS, the Black mafia, voices in his head, our mother's illness, our father's demands, and Jan's relentless threats. About a week or so before this I saw a telegram that Marvin had gotten from Jan telling him that he would never see his kids again as long as he lived. Little did she know how true that statement was because he never did see his kids again.*"

I felt like saying to Zeola that I would talk about suicide too if I carried all of those burdens on my shoulders. Gay Sr. would have been enough to send me over the edge, but of course I didn't tell her that. Instead, I asked her who in the family took the time to help Marvin with all of his issues, but she couldn't answer the question. Her only response was, "*I was too young and strung out on drugs myself, and so was everybody else.*"

I questioned Zeola about her statement that 'everybody' was strung out on drugs. I felt that that sounded a bit harsh. She then clarified that she was only talking about those working closest with Marvin while on tour.

"*When Marvin began to descend I watched but couldn't help him. Drugs had become as much a part of my life as his, and I was too young to recognize that we all needed help. We all became heavy cocaine users, which were so generously supplied by Marvin's new underground syndicate/promoters.*"

After hearing this, it was obvious that Marvin had nobody to turn to. There didn't seem to be a smart one in the bunch. However, I am sure that if Alberta had not been dealing with her own medical issues, she might have had the wherewithal to get him through his madness. That is, if Gay Sr. would have allowed it.

Now, by no means am I attempting to portray this man as a pathetic individual begging for someone to come along and save him from his problems. No, it appears that this situation was just the opposite. Marvin seemed to have a talent for going out of his way to destroy the very relationships that dared to try and get close to him. But that part of Marvin's personality seemed understandable to me. It indicated to me just how ingenious he probably was.

Zeola mentioned once that Marvin possessed a special ability to read people. I believe that statement went much deeper than even she realizes. I believe that this genius of a man read people so well that he could smell them coming before they even got to him. Whomever he encountered; whether it was to get him out of a jam or offer him work or supply him with drugs he knew that the bottom line was that they all wanted something from him, and I am sure that that did not make him feel good inside. So, being the strong person that he was he lashed out at everybody instead of holding in his feelings.

Imagine being so tuned into the human element that you can see vultures coming before they even get to you. And then imagine how it must have felt knowing that none of them really gave a damn about you as a person, but about what you could do for them in the end.

Marvin probably felt at a very early age that his mother was the only individual in his life capable of offering him unconditional love and affection, and that is why he was so devastated at the possibility of losing her to cancer. Aside from Alberta, the next closest person who seemed capable of possessing genuine affection for him was probably Zeola aka

"Sweetsie", the naive baby sister who stood by his side and helped him to the best of her ability. Unfortunately, her youth as well as her own drug habits and sexual misconduct hindered her ability to comprehend the magnitude of Marvin's discontentment. And it was no doubt that that discontentment was the very thing that blocked his ability to allow friends and associates such as Smokey and his attorney, Curtis Shaw, to help him.

Zeola believes that Marvin's fall from grace started with the promoters and their demands on him. She said that Marvin would call them up and curse them out and say things like, *"Yeah? Fuck you. Come and get me!"*

She said that she would think to herself, *"Marvin, please don't do this."* She felt that because he had accomplished everything that he could as an artist, she believed that he thought he had nothing to lose.

I understand how Zeola might have interpreted Marvin's feelings of accomplishments as being complete because that's the way it might seem for the average person, but Marvin was not an average person. He was a true musical genius, and nobody could possibly know what went on in his mind. She said herself that he loved mind games. Is it possible that the talk of suicide was a mind game? A game that was crying out for help as apposed to crying out for closure? It might seem that Marvin had done everything that he needed to do, but a true artist is seldom, if ever, finished with his/her work.

"The only thing that he missed was getting a star on the sidewalk in Hollywood, even though that's just politics. Everybody knows that you have to buy into that. Maybe Marvin didn't know that he had to literally buy the star. I wasn't aware of it until somebody told me. I always thought that it was like getting an award. I thought somebody like the Chamber of Commerce just gave

it to you because of your accomplishments. I guess almost everything is based on politics."

Marvin did get his Grammy award even though it took 20 years. And Zeola said that he did have a little bit of money after the IRS had been paid off. She said that she believes that Marvin finally felt that he had done all he could as an artist.

Zeola's belief that Marvin did not need to accomplish anything else in his lifetime was just unacceptable to me. Yes, I accept that maybe he felt down and out at times, which might have caused a lapse in his creativity, and I am fully aware of the possibility of paranoia due to his drug intake, but it still appears to me that he was reaching out for help, not for death.

Zeola said that she would not give the name of the promoter that was like the 'don' because some of the men are still alive, and she didn't want them to come after her. She did, however, want to give the name of the head of the organization because he is dead now, but I did not want to use his name. I am not interested in knowing these people. I am only concerned with what happened to Marvin, and why his father killed him.

"I think the promoter generally loved Marvin. He thought Marvin was a little difficult, but I think he liked that. He said that he didn't see that in a lot of Black people; probably because he didn't handle a lot of Black people. He liked Jan too. I was never able to put my finger on it, but they seemed like really good friends. He used to goose her whenever he got near her, and she never seemed to mind. She would just smile. It used to bother Marvin that Jan would let this man goose her. He would always ask me why I thought she let him do that to her. But I didn't have an answer to that question. I just knew that he didn't do it to me. I think he could tell that I didn't like things like that. I don't think he liked me. Maybe Jan was too scared to say 'no' to him. I don't know. We never talked about it."

Zeola said that when Marvin stepped into that situation he knew that he was stepping into something big time, but she thinks that Marvin didn't know just how bad it could get because he normally wasn't scared of anybody. And even after the realities began to set in he still stood up for himself.

"I never saw much interaction between Marvin and 'the man' because I didn't run in those circles. Marvin didn't want me around them. He felt that it was best that I not have that close familiarity with them. But I did associate myself with the Second Lieutenant and all of the ones under him. Marvin didn't know about that." Zeola smiled mischievously.

I give Zeola credit. At no time during these sessions did she ever attempt to cover up the fact that she was out there doing her thing as well. She did it all, and blamed nobody for it but herself. I believe that even though Marvin's intentions were to protect his baby sister from outside influences, he inadvertently dropped this young woman right down in the middle of a situation that was beyond even Marvin's comprehension.

"One day Marvin was shooting in the trees at the big house, so I asked Gary to go after him and of course Gary approached him from behind because he didn't know what Marvin would do with the gun. Gary said that Marvin was shooting and swearing that the mother-fuckers had stolen his money. He said that they had ruined his life. Marvin never adapted to somebody being in charge of him. This promoter was pretty powerful, and the way it was set up, he was in charge of everything. Gary finally got the gun from Marvin. Aside from me Gary was the only person who could talk to Marvin when he was like that."

***

Marvin had a reputation of not finishing tours, according to Zeola. She said that most of the time it was because of the lack of monies promised him.

"I think that the promoter was aware of Marvin's reputation so when he took over, I think he decided to hold Marvin's money until the shows were over. Instead he gave Marvin a gold credit card with which he could buy anything he wanted, but Marvin did not like that. He wanted cash. They bought him a house, but he wouldn't live in it. They bought him cars, but he wouldn't drive them. He would let Gary, me and anybody else who wanted to, drive them."

"Marvin's issue was 'Give me my money.'" Zeola explained.

"Maw and me were the only other people besides Marvin who could use the card. Jan couldn't even use it. And everybody was sick of us because we had a good time using it. We bought everything we wanted to buy. Marvin finally completed a whole tour to the end, and it was the best tour that I had been on. However, he did end up in the hospital because of fatigue."

Zeola said that she was there when Marvin was hospitalized. She said that the promoter's people felt that this was the best thing for Marvin. *"They had everything on Marvin looked at."* Marvin didn't go there to be treated for cocaine, but she said that they cleaned his nose and did whatever else is done for heavy cocaine users.

"Taking Marvin to the hospital was kept hush hush because of how the media reports things. Armed guards were at the door because they didn't want Jan there. They thought she would be a distraction for Marvin because every time she came around he would try to please her by doing cocaine with her heavier than usual."

This was another one of those times that Zeola's eyes lit up. She loved talking about Marvin and the good ole days. She was young and impressionable at that time, and loved the glamour and excitement that accompanied the tours.

"I only remember the promoter coming to Marvin's shows in San Francisco, San Diego and New York. And when he came it was laid out."

I asked Zeola what she meant by saying that everything was laid out, and she answered candidly.

"Backstage the Dom Perion was plentiful. The giant cocaine balls would be laid out for everybody. The backstage would be all laid out with food. And afterwards, the promoter would generally take everybody out to dinner. He always seemed so happy to see Marvin."

Shortly after that statement, I watched Zeola quickly retreat back into quietness. I knew instantly that she must have remembered something that brought her spirits down. I sat quietly and waited for her to finish her joint and gently place it in the ash tray. And then she spoke again.

"Shortly after Marvin returned from Europe he recorded the hit song, SEXUAL HEALING. And even though this song was a good thing, Marvin wasn't happy. Somehow he had gotten himself involved in a triangle of drugs, violence and organized crime."

Zeola sat quietly and took a few hits. I waited for her to continue.

"I remember being with Marvin backstage after a show when we spotted Eric, Marvin's sound engineer, leaning against the wall real pitiful-like. Marvin approached Eric and asked him what was wrong and he told Marvin that he had just been fired."

Zeola recalled seeing a combination of anger and confusion on Marvin's face.

"I think that Marvin just could not imagine anybody having the audacity to attempt such a move without his permission."

Zeola sat on the sofa with her shoes off and her feet tucked underneath her butt. The tension was so strong that I made sure not to say a word. Silence, until she spoke again.

"For the first time in my life I saw my strong big brother riddled with paranoia and powerlessness."

Zeola remembered Marvin excusing himself for a long while and then returning and informing Eric that he was still on the job.

"With much relief, we all got on the bus and returned to the motel. Well, everybody except Eric. It still remains a mystery how he got back to the motel before us. I suppose, like everybody else, I didn't pay attention to his absence since Marvin had assured us that everything was okay."

Zeola said that when they arrived at the motel they could hear agonizing screams of a woman. She said that they soon found out that it was Eric's girlfriend who was screaming because she had just found Eric's body hanging lifeless from the nozzle in the bathroom shower.

"I will never forget Marvin's face as he struggled to assist in removing the tightly knotted sweat pants from around Eric's neck. I remember waiting quietly with the rest of the group as Eric's limp body was gently placed on the cold tile floor."

After numerous attempts to resuscitate him, Eric still did not respond. He was later pronounced dead.

"If there was anybody who truly knew my brother, they knew that he was never a punk. Nobody controlled Marvin, not even Father. But suddenly someone else was in command of Marvin's life, and that was extremely difficult for him."

The police ruled Eric's death a suicide, but Marvin was convinced that it was murder. He told Zeola that he was convinced that he knew who had something to do with the killing, but Zeola wouldn't tell me any more than that. She said that she didn't want to get in trouble with anybody. She still believes that they would retaliate, even today. Instead, she

224

began to talk about something else. I knew that she was changing the subject, and I did not have a problem with it.

***

"The tour was promoted, the money was collected and Marvin was threatened if he didn't do the shows."

At the end of Marvin's last tour in 1983 Zeola said that Marvin had made over ten million dollars, but only received one million. Marvin told her that the promoters took the rest of the money.

"Marvin used his portion of the money to pay off debts, help the family, and support his drug habits. He was broke, and there was nothing he could do about it. He told me that he was tired and disgusted, but he knew that if he became rebellious against anyone, they might possibly take the life of one of his family members, and he did not want that to happen. Eric's death was enough for him."

Some of her memories with Marvin seemed to bring Zeola's spirits down, but she still continued to reminisce about them. It was during these times that I was sure that the marijuana helped her cope.

She remembered one night when she was over at a band member's house that she dated, and as usual, Zeola said that she was trying to hide what she was doing from Marvin because he didn't want her hanging around the band. She said that Marvin called Robin's house looking for her.

"She knew that I was over this guy's house so she told him that she didn't know. Marvin convinced Robin that it was a matter of life or death so she told on me. So he told her to call there and to tell me to call him. So when Robin called and told me that Marvin wanted me to call him at Maw's house I panicked. When I called Marvin he told me to go home and get my gun and then come over to Ma's house because my life was in intimate danger. That tripped me out. I will never forget it."

Zeola said that it was at least 1 o'clock in the morning. So she got in her car and on her way home she was sure that this van was following her.

"I was so paranoid it was just unbelievable. When I turned the van turned. All I could hear in my head was 'intimate danger' until I got to Marvin. That van seemed to follow me all the way from Silver Lake to Highland Avenue. I was living at Olympic and Hauser at that time. And I flew home the rest of the way."

When Zeola got home she said that she called Marvin and he told her to call Gary and tell him to bring his daughter and her to the big house because he trusted Gary.

"Gary and I weren't together at this time. So I told Gary that Marvin wanted him to come and get me and take me to the big house. So Gary got up and was there in a few minutes. He didn't live too far away. In the meantime, Marvin had told me not to turn on any lights in the house. So I was sitting and looking out the window in the dark with my gun in my hand. I was scared to death. So Prince, my neighbor, happened to be coming around the house on my grass and the only reason I didn't shoot him was because I couldn't figure out how to use the damn gun. Anyway, after I didn't shoot Prince and everything, he offered to ride with us to the big house for support. So he got in the car with us. I was halfway lying down in the back seat because I was so scared. I really tripped hard. Marvin had really scared the shit out of me. So all the way to the big house Gary was calm and assuring me that nothing was going to happen to me because I was with him. Gary didn't really like Prince because he knew that Prince liked me, so I think he was letting Prince know that he was taking care of me that night."

When they pulled up to the house Zeola said that Marvin was hanging out of her father's bedroom window yelling, *"Run! Run as fast as you can!"* So they ran like crazy from the car to the house.

"We all ran into the house one by one as Marvin watched out for us. Every time Marvin would yell, 'Now!' another one of us would run from the car to the big house."

Zeola said that Marvin had placed metal utensils and empty tin cans in every window of the big house so that if anybody ever tried to break in, it would make noise by falling to the floor.

"Well, once we all got in the house it turned out that Marvin had been talking to the promoter and must have felt threatened because they had told him before that they would kill his family if he didn't cooperate, and I guess that's what was happening now. Marvin really had a problem with authority and he could not get past the fact that the promoters never gave him his money."

Zeola said she thinks that Marvin must have threatened somebody and was in fear of retaliation.

"He never told me exactly what went down. I'm still not sure if Marvin had been going through a bout with paranoia, or if we had been truly threatened by anybody. But he wasn't real happy when he found out that they wouldn't give him all of his money."

Zeola reiterated how Marvin would tell you to kiss his ass, fuck you or go to hell in a second. He would say, *"I'm here! Come and get me!"* She said that she didn't know what Marvin had said to these guys this time, but it must have been enough to make him feel the need to gather everybody in the family together.

"Marvin was really upset about his money, but regardless of what this was about, none of us slept well that night."

By now, I was so intrigued by Zeola's 'mystery tale' that I barely noticed that the audio tape was about to run out, so I quickly stopped the recorder, flipped the tape over to the 'B' side and pushed 'record' and 'play' in a matter of seconds.

227

I thought about the fact that this could have turned out to be one of the most deadly massacres in the history of Hollywood if someone was really out to destroy Marvin's family. But because of my sometimes distorted sense of humor and vivid imagination, I immediately envisioned this to be one of the funniest comedies of error that one could imagine due to the fact that it could have very well been a figment of Marvin's drug-induced imagination. I apologize for my sense of humor, but when Zeola finished her story I just didn't know whether to laugh or cry. I began to imagine Marvin yelling out the window, and the family running in fast motion, tripping over one another like the Keystone cops in an old Charley Chan movie. All — for no reason.

However, the look on Zeola's face quickly told me that she would not have appreciated my sense of humor, so I fought back the laughter, and proceeded to do my job, which was to write the story.

Looking back on that session I remember recognizing the fact that I had only one of two choices; either make light of the situation or break down and cry uncontrollably for the sake of this dear man who was probably experiencing a level of distress both mentally and emotionally beyond all comprehension. Fortunately, the all-out Mafioso type massacre did not occur, and the family was safe from harm.

I never got a chance to ask Zeola where her father was during that harrowing experience. And I dare not try to guess.

***

Listening to Zeola sometimes felt like a child being told an amazing bedtime story that never seemed to end.

At one point Zeola said that Marvin had considered the ministry, but then she said that he had decided that he had already accomplished a lot in that area because he had reached so many people through the healing powers of his music so he didn't address that issue anymore.

"*Many fans had told Marvin about how much his music helped them get through hard times or sad times. So he did accept that he was doing God's will in that way. And he got a great deal of spiritual satisfaction out of it.*"

By now I was starting to feel a bit confused. I wasn't sure if I wanted to continue writing this story because it was not going in the direction that I anticipated. I began feeling a combination of helplessness and guilt. Helplessness because I had become so caught up in this project that I started wishing that I had been there to help this man even though I didn't know him personally. And then there is the guilt that I was feeling for exposing intimate details of Marvin's personal life. Was I doing the right thing?

I sat a moment to think about why I had decided to complete a book that was literally dragging me in a direction that I was not prepared to go. Zeola had already told me that she had changed her mind about completing it so I wondered if I was doing it out of vengeance because I had lost a year and a half of income, or was I just being a typical selfish writer wanting to get my work recognized. Finally, I made the decision to stop this madness and not write another page, but then something happened that changed my mind; the blinking lights.

That day I turned off my computer, decided to take my mind away from everything by preparing my clothes for the following work week. I went to my closest to figure out what I was going to wear. I've always hated ironing so I try to get all of it done on the weekend so that I don't have to worry about it during the week. Nothing is worse for me than getting up to go to work and all of a sudden you have to iron something. That starts my day off so totally wrong.

My walk-in closet is a comfortable sized little room which has been reorganized with shelves for shoes and the proper bars for dresses, tops and bottoms. But even with all of the proper bells and whistles, the closet is still a mess. So before opening its double doors I paused for a very brief moment to prepare myself for the mess inside. I knew that I would have to step over a few things to get to the hanging rod of dresses straight ahead of me, or kick everything aside to reach the pants, skirts and blouses to my right. I didn't even consider looking to my left because I always hang the off-season stuff over there, plus, a messy pile of dirty clothes that I planned to wash that afternoon separated me from that area.

So, I opened the closet door and to my surprise before I could even flick on the light switch, the forty watt light bulb, hanging from the middle of the ceiling in my intimate little closet suddenly burst a blinding kilowatt of piercing light in my face as if attempting to destroy the very cornea of my eyes. Shocked, I quickly covered my face with my hands to avoid any further damage, but the pain from the unexpected burst of light had already traveled to my brain. It only took a few seconds to gain control of myself, and when I removed my hands from my eyes the unlit 40 watt bulb came back on and then flickered about five times and went out. Just as quickly as this started, it ended, and my closet was dark, and I was somewhat distressed to say the least. Based on previous paranormal experiences I knew that that was a sign to continue with my work and not be discouraged. And that is what I did without question, and I am sure that I made the right decision.

***

Gay Sr. only participated in one of Marvin's shows that Zeola said she knows of, and that was in Washington DC However, she said that she would not put it past him to have come without telling anybody. She said that she could see him possibly standing somewhere where he couldn't be seen.

"Father always had an excuse not to come to Marvin's concerts. Either his back hurt or he didn't want to fly because he was afraid of airplanes or whatever he could think up, but Maw always came. She loved the whole idea of Marvin being a star. This gave her a chance to go places and wear mink coats. She was finally being treated like a queen. So, once again, my father became jealous. He would throw up mean things to her. He would say that she acted like Marvin was her husband. He accused her of running off to be with Marvin instead of staying home with him."

I thought to myself that I would have gone with Marvin too. Staying home with that man would have been totally out of the question.

"The news media blamed our dysfunctional family for the death of Marvin. They would prefer to believe that we were so greedy, selfish and controlling that it was only destined that my father would actually murder my brother. While our family may not have lived a typical lifestyle it was not my family that led to my brother's untimely death. I know better than anyone why my brother died, and I am the only person alive who can accurately share that information with Marvin's fans."

Zeola continues to believe that Marvin planned his own death. I continue to believe that he did not want to die. He just wanted peace, but was surrounded by malevolence.

I did not agree with the fact that Marvin felt that he had accomplished everything because I don't believe that any true artist ever stops wanting to create. It's in the blood. I believe that Marvin would have had so much more to live for if he could have just found the peace that he so vehemently craved.

***

"The world seemed sad through Marvin's eyes. Not only did Jan bar him from seeing his children because he had pressed charges against her for attempted murder, but other death threats unfolded through time."

Zeola told me that Marvin had been receiving death threats while on one of their tours, and they were not coming from Jan or anybody that they knew personally. She said that it was suspected that the Black mafia was involved, so they prepared for the worse.

"I soon found myself, along with several crewmembers, guarding Marvin's performances backstage with machine guns and pistols. I can't imagine what I must have looked like walking around carrying a high-powered weapon that was almost as big as I was; not to mention how much my hands shook due to the fact that I didn't know what the hell I was doing. And the drugs in my system did not help matters. However, I am sure I would have figured it out quickly enough if the occasion arose because I was not about to let anything happen to my big brother."

In addition, she said that after Marvin became famous Gay Sr. started taping all of Marvin's telephone conversations with their mother whenever he called home. Zeola said that her mother would tell her that Doc was taping them. Zeola also remembered being on the road with Marvin, and he would be on the telephone with their mother, and Marvin would tell her that Gay Sr. was taping him at that time. So Marvin knew about it also.

"Father had started accusing Marvin and my mom of having more of a relationship than just mother and son. But it never happened. There was never anything between them other than

232

everlasting love between a mother and her son. This created a lot of hostility in our household. And I think that that was the beginning of the end for Marvin and my father because Father was determined to catch the two of them talking about more than mother and son stuff."

All that I could think of at this moment was that Gay Sr.'s mind probably went in that direction because of his own despicable actions in the past with other women and possibly his own daughter. I say this because Zeola told me once that she might have been molested as a teenager. But when asked more about it, her inability to confirm or deny that it was her father was interesting. She told me that she wasn't sure who did it. She said that she thinks that it may have been her father or his brother. She wasn't sure. She claimed to have lost a portion of her memory during her teenage years.

Zeola told me about the birth of a little girl that may have been the result of the possible molestation. She said that everybody says that the girl looks just like her, but she would not acknowledge that this was, in fact, her child. All of this seemed vague to me. I just couldn't figure out where she was going with this conversation. I wasn't sure if it was the weed talking because she had smoked several joints that day or if she was really trying to tell me something that was difficult to reveal. So I asked her to clarify what she was trying to say, and she immediately changed the subject and refused to readdress it. I think she decided that it was not something she should have been talking about. Maybe it was for the sake of the child, maybe it was in defense of her father, I don't know. Regardless of the reason I totally respected her decision and did not address it again. So she changed the subject, and we moved on.

***

"My father just couldn't accept Marvin's success over his, and he wasn't going down easily." Zeola said as she lowered her head and reached for a joint.

Zeola told me that after her father went to jail she found some audio tapes that he had recorded but she would not tell me what was on them. At first I assumed that the tapes involved conversations between Marvin and his mother because Zeola had already said that her father had been taping Marvin's telephone calls while he was on tour, but that was not what was on those tapes, according to Zeola. Evidently the recordings involved conversations between Marvin and his father. She said that the two of them really went at it, which made me even more curious so I asked her what she had done with them. I thought maybe I could convince her at some point to let me hear them, but she said that she didn't have them anymore.

"I destroyed the tapes about two years after Marvin died. I took everything out of Father's room when he went to jail. I felt that nobody else should ever hear them. The tapes were foul. The alcohol was doing just as much damage to Father as the drugs was doing to Marvin."

Zeola said that the things that were said on those tapes between her brother and her father should be kept between her brother and her father. That's how serious she said they were. The only thing that she told me was that her father thought that her mother was too close to Marvin. All that I could think of with that statement was that Gay Sr. probably had those thoughts because of the things that he had done in his lifetime. I still wasn't sure if he had molested Zeola. I have learned over the years that usually the person who harbors the most jealousy is the one who has done the most dirt.

Speaking of dirt, Zeola said that all of her father's brothers have done something bad in their lives. She said they were either in jail for killing somebody or robbing somebody.

"Father was the only one left in the family that was respectable. He was a minister; he had nice kids, a good wife, and had made it in DC. They all looked up to my father."

I don't suppose his brothers knew about the allegations of cross-dressing as well as stretching his kids out on their beds naked and beating them with big leather straps, or smacking a small child's hands so hard that they bled, all because she didn't say her abc's correctly. I wonder what they thought about him after he shot and killed his own son in cold blood. No, it doesn't appear that this man was much different from the rest of his siblings. What does seem obvious is that most of their unconventional behavior probably emanated from those supposedly dreadful slave mentality beatings carried out by Gay Sr.'s mother.

CHAPTER
19

NO TIME TO GRIEVE

"I wasn't there when they took Father away. I was at the hospital with Gary waiting to hear from the doctors about Marvin when the word got out that Marvin was dead. You could hear people everywhere screaming, 'No, no.' The screams were unbelievable. I will never forget it. It was like a chain reaction at the hospital, and it seemed like it lasted a long time. People everywhere were hollering and crying out loud. Some were almost hysterical."

Zeola said that when she got back to the big house her mother was still in the rocking chair.

"I went in to her and told her that Marvin didn't make it. She cried and shook her head. It wasn't a hysterical cry, but probably the saddest cry anybody could make without being hysterical. Her heart was truly broken."

The entire family went to the police station together. *"That's when one of Marvin's bodyguards came up to me and said that my father needed help, and that I should be the one to do it. So, it was all on me. I had to find Father a lawyer and everything. So, I left Maw at the police station and Jeanne took care of her."*

When they got back to the big house Zeola said that people were there taking things out of the house, so Gary put a stop to that.

"He put everybody out of the house that didn't belong there. But somebody had turned on one of Marvin's records in another part of the house, so I screamed, 'Turn that record off!' That was the only time I remember loosing control. I just couldn't bear to hear his voice. It was just too much for me. I must have screamed for them to turn if off at least three times before they heard me. I still don't know who that was."

Zeola said that she went up to Marvin's room and picked up the straw hat that he had worn everyday since he had been back, and she put it on her head and then sat on the side of the bed in the same spot where he always sat when he woke up.

"Marvin would sit in that same spot sometimes for twenty or thirty minutes before he would get up and go into the bathroom."

As Zeola sat there, she said that she felt his spirit through that hat.

"It gave me the strength to do what I had to do, which was to take care of all of the arrangements and stuff. For a brief moment I sat there wondering why me. I mean I was the youngest in the family. I was the baby! I wanted so badly to say, 'Come on guys, I'm the baby!' Frankie couldn't do much because Marvin had basically died in his arms and Jeanne was taking care of Maw."

Not long after Zeola and Gary got back to the house a man from the Black Mafia came over to meet with Gary. Zeola remembered that his name was Ernie. She said that he told Gary that he had heard that Marvin trusted in him and used him for a lot of things, but Gary instantly developed a dislike for this man.

"I remember sitting on the side of Marvin's bed with his straw hat still on my head, and Ernie started looking around. I remember him asking me if the police had found anything, and he asked if the house was clean. I knew that he was referring to drugs because he had mentioned the bag of cocaine. So I shook my head and said, 'No.' He must have believed me because he finally left the house, and we didn't see him again."

Zeola said that she made all the arrangements for the funeral and didn't have a lot of time to grieve or anything because Marvin's death was so sudden. She said that she didn't even attend the scattering of his ashes.

"I just could not say goodbye. The service was videotaped for me, but I haven't looked at it yet."

When Marvin died she said that everything fell in her lap.

"I was the one who had to go to the hospital and get the official announcement, go to the police station, and then make the official

announcement. I had Robin call Don Joe because I needed to know what kind of money we were working with, and I was told to go ahead and get whatever I needed and not to worry about the cost. To me, he didn't answer my question about the money. He just said to get whatever I needed. So that's what I did. My landlady helped me write the obituary and I got a picture for her to put on it. I put the whole program together, decided who I wanted to speak and what minister I wanted to use, and where we were going to have it. I picked out a beautiful casket that was just for cremation. I decided to dress Marvin in his admiral outfit that he liked and performed in. He loved that outfit. I decided that I wanted the band to play the overture used at his concerts."

After the funeral the casket was taken over to the cremation part of forest lawn.

"I believe that Dick Gregory went with it. I didn't go. As far as I was concerned I was done with it. I did not want to deal with his cremation. That was too final for me."

Later on Zeola claimed to have discovered that Jan had kept some of Marvin's ashes, and her kids were wearing his ashes around their necks.

"Well, that was the grossest thing to me at that time. I couldn't understand why somebody would wear a dead person's ashes around their neck. But I was young and didn't understand."

Shortly after the funeral Zeola said that she became Gay Sr.'s power of attorney.

"I ended up having to make all the decisions with the lawyers, deal with my father's operation and handle the court dates as well as making decisions about his bail. Again, I'm not really having time to grieve about Marvin like the rest of the family."

Zeola said that she was sad and her heart was broken, but she knew she had to help her father. She felt that helping him

239

did not mean that she condoned what he did, but she did understand it.

"I knew that Marvin wanted out."

She said that Marvin knew that if he had done anything even close to physically touching or pushing or hitting her father or her mother, as passive and loving as Alberta was, they would have killed him.

"It was bad enough talking back to either of them. And Marvin knew that gun was in the house. Nobody on the outside was threatening to kill Marvin at this time, and he was not going to take his own life. So I believe that he pushed my father to that point so that my father would kill him. And as far as my father was concerned, he was defending himself. He was afraid for his life. Not knowing that Marvin had literally put him in a position to feel that way."

Zeola said that her mother told her that Marvin basically told Gay Sr. that if he didn't kill him that he would basically kill Gay Sr. To me the word 'basically' does not mean that Marvin said those very words. And no place on the audio tapes did I hear her say that her mother definitely said that Marvin threatened to kill his father if his father did not do it first. So I questioned her, and she replied.

"Marvin may not have said those exact words, but my father took what he said to mean that. Marvin was a powerful man. I do believe that if Father hadn't shot Marvin, that Marvin probably would have continued to put enough fear into Father until he did kill him. And in Marvin's warped mind there's probably no other way he would have probably wanted to go. The man who brought him into this world was the man who took him out. I believe that in Marvin's mind this was a mercy killing. My father never really understood all of this, and he kind of blocked everything out and went into something like Alzheimer's where he just didn't remember

any of it. That's why I helped him. Nobody understood what Marvin was going through but me, and maybe my mother. But even my mother didn't know how deep this thing was with him. Nobody knew how really bad he wanted to be away from what was going on in his life. Marvin was not afraid of death. He knew that he would be at peace."

Zeola's firm belief that Marvin had literally planned to have his father murder him, bothered my deeply. And the family's inability to help Marvin sickened me even more because if they all knew that Marvin was that desperate for peace and affection, yet did little if anything to help him, then I say *"God help that family."*

I am aware that right up to his death Marvin's problems seemed to be insurmountable. But look at this from another point of view. Here he had someone whom he 'loved unconditionally' keeping away his most precious possessions, his children 'for the sake of money', and another person whom he 'loved unconditionally' refusing to give him the one thing he needed most, a simple hug and an ounce of praise for being the talented genius that he had become, and the rest of those whom he 'loved unconditionally' just hanging on for whatever material things they could get from him. How lonely is that? Here is a man who could give the world such beautiful music, but he could not find peace without death. How sad is that?

"As I have said before, my father could be very mean; especially when he drank. I don't know if Father had been drinking the day he killed Marvin, but I don't think a drink would have mattered because Marvin did put his hands on Father. And my father never said he was sorry until that last day in court when the judge was ready to sentence him. The judge asked him if he had anything to say, and

241

Father said that he was sorry that he had killed his son, but he felt that he had to do it."

Zeola said that when you looked at Gay Sr. on the television after Marvin's death you could see no remorse.

"He looked hard, and if you knew my father like I know him, he was feeling justified. He had said 'My son was getting ready to hurt me. My baby that I held, my seed, was getting ready to harm me, and I couldn't let him do that. Father didn't know that Marvin had sent the rest of the guns out of the house accept the one that Father had. My father didn't know Marvin might have been going back to the room to get a gun and might come back and shoot him. That's why his sentence was reduced to manslaughter as opposed to first degree murder. It wasn't premeditated. He did that out of fear for his life. Like I said before, Marvin put enough fear in my father to make him believe that if he didn't kill Marvin, that Marvin would probably end up hurting him; even though Marvin never would do that. But Marvin had to make my father believe that."

For a brief moment after that adamant statement about her opinion of the killing, Zeola sat thinking with an expression of bitterness. Of course I waited patiently to hear what she had to say because she had mentioned earlier that her father knew that all of the guns were gone because she said that Gary told her that Gay Sr. had requested to keep one of them. So I waited for her to clarify her statement, but instead, she moved on to something else.

"The writer, David Ritz, tried to put himself in my father's shoes when he wrote about us. He doesn't even know my father. I had to think for both Marvin and Father in order to understand all of this. I basically knew what Marvin's thoughts were, but I didn't quite understand my father's thoughts. I knew where Marvin wanted to be because Marvin played a form of chess with my father. Once he found out that my mother had cancer, Marvin probably

knew that it had to be my father who would kill him. After I explained all of this to my mother she understood and agreed with me. My father had never been to prison before. He had never even been arrested for a traffic ticket."

I suppose I will always have a hard time understanding Zeola's analogy of Marvin's death. Yes, Gay Sr. might not have been imprisoned before, and maybe he hadn't gotten any parking tickets, but when a man beats his kids naked, and express such resentment and jealousy toward his own son, not to mention the cross dressing and wigs; he had some serious problems. And I don't believe that he needed to shoot and kill Marvin over any type of family squabble. And after listening to these numerous hours of tapes, I don't believe that Marvin set his father up to commit this heinous crime. But, that's just my opinion.

After Marvin's death Zeola said that she and Gary had taken possession of Marvin's drugs.

"We did cocaine every kind of way you could think to do it. And even though we put it in water and dripped it down our nose, we put it in cigarettes, we still weren't getting high because I was so depressed and was grieving so much. I really thought the drugs were helping me cope. Every time I went to court for my father, I think I was loaded. Gary and I would get high going to the courthouse. I felt it helped me deal with the people and the press and the magazines. I wouldn't be as shy. Going through the court dates was not easy, especially when I found out that my father had a brain tumor."

It could not have been easy for Zeola, I am sure, and I respect the fact that she took care of her father's needs. But one can only imagine how all of this might have played out without the influence of drugs. I am sure that this entire story would have gone in another direction. There might not even be a story because Marvin might still be with us today.

243

"After my father passed away, I went to Shelton who is like a Bishop now because I knew that the church still loved Father. Before Maw died he was around her a lot. We had a lot of problems because Shelton seemed to only come around to get money from my mother, like tithes for the church. Maw still believed in that religion, but she was sick. And when it got to the point where my mother was really really sick and had no more money to give him, he didn't come around anymore. And when the Jehovah's Witness started coming around and talking to her and praying with her and spending time with her, they opened her eyes to see that the Bishop's church wasn't really for her."

Zeola said that when her mom passed away, she did not want Shelton to preside over her service.

"How dare he come around for money, and then when she was really sick, he wasn't there. He kept saying that "Mother Gay would have wanted him to do the funeral, but I knew better, and I told him no. So my sister tried to get another minister of the same religion. Shelton tried to stop all the other ministers from doing it. But finally my sister found someone who was willing to preside over the service."

When Zeola saw the first television show about Marvin on A&E, and they had the holiness church there and Shelton and his wife were sitting there talking like they had been at my mother's side every single day, she said that she got very angry. *"And they were saying that my father had talked to them. I was furious because my father didn't talk to anybody about anything. Nobody. Nothing."*

Several years later Zeola said that she was at a swap meet with her daughter, Nikki, and she heard somebody say, *"Sweetsie!"* She said that it was Shelton's wife, Baby Sis. *"So we hugged."*

Zeola said that she tried to let bygones be bygones.

"I tried not to hold grudges because I'm not supposed to. I might not always forget, but I can forgive. I've got to forgive because that's what God wants."

She said that she hadn't seen or talked to that couple since her mom passed. She said that she didn't see them again until Gay Sr. died.

"I called Shelton and told him that my father had passed away. He said that he would call the church and see if they would handle the funeral. I told him that we didn't have any money and that there was no insurance. So he called the bishop who had been my father's rival, and they said that they would pay for the funeral as long as it was under a certain amount. So Shelton went with me to pick out the casket and to choose the gravesite and we found a chapel. I remember thinking about the fact that here I was again handling a funeral for my family. I wondered what is going to happen when I pass away. Who is going to take care of me? After that Shelton told me that he still loved me, and I told him that I love him too. Since then we have talked. He has helped me out a couple of times when I had financial problems. One time he paid to have my electricity on."

Zeola said that she still has problems when she sees these people talking as if they were so close to Marvin, or when they act like they really knew him.

"I remember Little Richard saying that he was at the big house shortly after the shooting, and claimed that blood was everywhere. That was not true. There wasn't anybody in that house unless he was one of the people stealing things. And I don't think he would do that. Shortly after we left the house behind the ambulance to go to the hospital, Robin came to the house and said that the police didn't allow anybody else in the house. We even had to have a police escort in order to get back into the house after we left the police station. So anybody who says that they were there at any time during the shooting is lying or was stealing. And Little Richard's comment

about 'blood being everywhere' was also a lie. Marvin got shot in the chest and the bullets did not go in one side and come out the other side and cause a lot of blood to spatter. That did not happen"

When Gary and Frankie carried Marvin down the steps Zeola said that there was no blood dripping anywhere.

"We did not have to clean up a lot of blood. I was so pissed when I heard this on the David Ritz show. All of those people were just trying to get in the limelight. I hated it. And I am now prepared to set the record straight; to put closure to all of this. Nobody was there when Marvin was shot, but my mother and my father. And nobody arrived shortly thereafter except the family, the police, Robin and the thieves."

I am sure that I speak for many of Marvin's fans when I say that my heart goes out to the Gay family and their loss of this great human being. I suppose it is easy for those of us who were not privy to Marvin's personal life to sit back and comment on what could have been or what should have been, but we must all be reminded at all times that God is the only true judge.

My heart goes out to the remaining Gay family members and friends. It truly was an unforgettable era of WHAT'S GOING ON and SEXUAL HEALING.

Because this was my last chapter, I felt quite comfortable in having my radio on, and as soon as I completed this last paragraph I could hear Marvin's voice on the radio singing LET'S GET IT ON, which I consider to be my confirmation.

AP Images/Lennox McLendon

Marvin and Bubbie
London, 1980

247

AUTHOR'S NOTES

Audrey Lewis is one of the few women to join the elite circle of independent filmmakers. She wrote, directed and produced a motion picture entitled THE GIFTED. This blend of fictional and real characters won her an induction in the Black Filmmakers Hall of Fame for her screenplay and picture in 1994.

In 1997 she produced another award winning feature film, A MOMENT OF ROMANCE for Hong Kong, China. Since that time she has written a fictional novel, BIG MAMMA AND CELESTE, a tale of victimization and sexual abuse.

Although her Bachelor of Science degree in Business Management has taught her how to survive in the every day work place, her most memorable studies were at the Art Institute of Pittsburgh.

Her ability to combine her literary talent with her undeniable spirituality, as well as the love and respect for the musical genius, Marvin, has allowed her to give a clear and close-up view of who Marvin was, how he lived, and why he died, as told to her by his sister Zeola Gaye.